Everyday Ethics in Real Estate

Doris Barrell, GRI, DREI, CDEI

Dearborn™

Real Estate Education

This publication is designed to provide accurate and authoritative information in regard to the subject matter covered. It is sold with the understanding that the publisher is not engaged in rendering legal, accounting, or other professional advice. If legal advice or other expert assistance is required, the services of a competent professional should be sought.

President: Dr. Andrew Temte
Chief Learning Officer: Dr. Tim Smaby
Executive Director, Real Estate Education: Melissa Kleeman-Moy
Development Editor: Evonna Burr

EVERYDAY ETHICS IN REAL ESTATE
©2014 Kaplan, Inc.
Published by DF Institute, Inc., d/b/a Dearborn Real Estate Education
332 Front St. S., Suite 501
La Crosse, WI 54601

Printed in the United States of America

ISBN: 978-1-4754-2558-1 / 1-4754-2558-9
PPN: 3200-5176

contents

Although ethics has been an important issue for real estate practitioners for many years, it has gained greater attention since 2000, when the National Association of REALTORS® mandated quadrennial ethics training for all members of the association. In addition, many states now include a course in ethics as a requirement for initial licensure as well as part of the curriculum for continuing education courses required for license renewal.

Dearborn Real Estate Education's original ethics book, *Ethics and Real Estate,* was frequently used to meet NAR requirements, both in the classroom and online. For the second quadrennial period for mandated NAR training, *Ethics in Today's Real Estate World* was designed with a new look at ethics and the real estate professional. Prior to creating this course, real estate industry educators and practitioners answered survey questions concerning the content of the new book. Their collective insight into important ethics issues of today helped form the framework of this book and its many features.

In 2010, *Know the Code: Real Estate Ethics* was updated to meet the NAR requirements for the third quadrennial mandatory ethics training period. This edition of the ethics book, *Everyday Ethics in Real Estate,* not only includes the latest updates, but also features additional case studies and real-life examples.

Everyday Ethics in Real Estate begins with a chapter on ethics that focuses on ethical situations seen in today's boardrooms, classrooms, and locker rooms and the impact they have on the public's attitude to ethics in general. In Chapter 2, the ethics concepts have been expanded to include a view of ethical business practices from various real estate disciplines. Colleagues from several other specialties, ranging from appraisal to property management, provided input on how they see ethics as a part of their daily practice. The coverage of the National Association of REALTORS® Code of Ethics has been expanded in this book to include commentary and examples on all of the articles of the Code in Chapter 3.

A code of ethics has limited meaning unless there is a system in place for enforcement of the tenets of the Code. Chapter 4 describes the enforcement process and includes actual case studies reproduced from the *2014 NAR Code of Ethics and Arbitration Manual.* Beginning around the turn of this century, many areas of the United States found themselves in what is known as a hot real estate market. This was then followed by a sharp decline in the overall housing market and resulting economic crisis in the mortgage financing industry. Whether a hot or cold market, overwhelming changes in the real estate world can lead to aggressive behavior, which often results in unethical business practices. Many of these phenomena are described in Chapter 5.

Chapter 6 discusses the four ethical paradigms first seen in *Ethics and Real Estate,* with additional insight on the principles by which ethical decisions are made, from the writings of Rushworth Kidder, noted ethics scholar and lecturer and founder of the Institute for Global Ethics. No two cases are ever identical. Circumstances vary, people have their own particular idiosyncrasies, and the overall atmosphere of the local marketplace differs. Ultimately, someone has to make a final decision.

By reading and discussing the material and the case studies in this text, you will be better prepared the next time you are faced with your own ethical dilemma!

Doris Barrell, GRI, DREI, CDEI, has been in the real estate business for over 30 years, working first for a builder-developer, then as a general brokerage agent, and for 9 years as managing broker for a 60-agent office in Alexandria, Virginia. She has brought this wealth of real-life experience into the classroom and her writing on the subjects of real estate finance, agency, fair housing, ethics, diversity, and legal and legislative issues.

In addition to *Everyday Ethics in Real Estate*, Doris is author of *Real Estate Finance Today, Ethics and Real Estate, Ethics in Today's Real Estate World,* and *Know the Code: Real Estate Ethics;* coauthor of *Essentials of Real Estate Finance;* and contributing editor for *Real Estate Fundamentals, Reverse Mortgages for Seniors,* and *Virginia Real Estate Practice and Law,* all published by Dearborn Real Estate Education. Most recently, she has prepared numerous online courses for continuing education in many states throughout the country.

Doris developed the *Expanding Housing Opportunities* course for NAR, which she both taught and trained other trainers. She spent many years as a teaching consultant for the International Real Property Foundation, bringing real estate education to countries in Eastern Europe and Southeast Asia. Additionally, Doris served for 13 years as a senior instructor for NeighborWorks® America, preparing course materials and leading training sessions at NWA Institutes held in cities throughout the United States.

chapter one

3 hour ethics once you get license

Ethics in Today's World

Learning Objectives

Upon completion of this chapter, you will be able to

■ discuss the difference between ethics, morality, and the law and the impact that corporate scandals have on the public's attitude toward ethics in the business world;

■ outline specific guidelines for ethical business practice and give examples of professional associations that provide a code of ethics for their members; and

■ describe ethical issues that exist in the classroom and in the sports world today and how they are being addressed.

■ Key Terms

AACSB	ethics	SEC
Big Four	morality	situational ethics

■ Introduction

Ethics—the word echoes off the walls of the boardroom, the classroom, the locker room—but what does it mean? Ethics may be a buzzword of the day, but it is also one of the oldest topics of discussion. From Socrates teaching in a fifth century BC Greek forum to the U.S. Congress holding hearings on the use of steroids in sports, people have talked about ethics and ethical behavior. How important is it to do the right thing? And is the right thing always the same in all circumstances? And who decides what is right anyway? Can it be as simple as this quote from Oprah Winfrey?

"Real integrity is doing the right thing, knowing that nobody's going to know whether you did it or not."

1. Learning Objective: Discuss the difference between ethics, morality, and the law and the impact that corporate scandals have on the public's attitude toward ethics in the business world.

■ Ethics, Morality, and the Law

The first question to be asked in the study of ethics is whether *ethics* and *morality* mean the same thing. A number of philosophy professors would argue that they are synonymous, but others define them differently. Some might argue that ethics are rules set down by man, whereas morals come from a higher being. In 1836, Ralph Waldo Emerson said that, "Ethics and religion differ herein, that the one is the system of human duties commencing from man, the other, from God. Religion includes the personality of God, ethics does not."

One inherent problem with equating ethics and morality is that the standards of morality as set by different religions may vary. Would this mean that ethical behavior would also have many variations? If so, this is getting very close to accepting the concept of *situational ethics,* where behavior may always be determined by the circumstances.

Albert Schweitzer tried to simplify the definition of ethics by saying, "Ethics, too, are nothing but reverence for life. That is what gives me the fundamental principle of morality, namely, that good consists in maintaining, promoting, and enhancing life, and that destroying, injuring, and limiting life are evil."

Just as ethics and morality are not synonymous, neither are ethics and law. Laws can be learned, mandated, and enforced, but no one has ever been able to legislate a sense of ethical behavior. In many cases, ethics go beyond the limitations of the law. The law draws a firm black-and-white line between right and wrong, while ethics tend to come in multiple shades of gray. An ethical dilemma is often likely to be a case of right versus right. When Joe breaks into Wal-Mart to steal a television, it's pretty obvious it is a case of right versus wrong. But is it less obvious when Jim breaks into the corner grocery store to steal bread and water for his family in flood-soaked New Orleans? Therein lies the dilemma.

If a sense of ethics or morality does not come naturally, must it be learned? Or is it all merely a matter of conscience? Does every person have an inner sense of what is right and what is wrong and the ability to always do the right thing? Mark Twain said, "Morals are an acquirement—like music, like a foreign language, like piety, poker, paralysis—no man is born with them."

■ Ethics and the Boardroom

Headlines of major newspapers throughout America today often present a grim picture of corporate ethics. Take the initiative to read headlines and articles about corporate scandals that appear on the front page or business section of your local newspaper or in the Drudge Report or other online news services. It comes as no surprise that the American public is highly suspicious of big business today and has lost faith in the stock market. Specific names have been eliminated in the following headlines, but they may be recognized by readers of this text:

"Top Bank Offers $2 Billion to Settle Enron-Related Claims"

"Major Healthcare Provider to Pay $100 Million to Settle Fraud Charges with SEC"

"Top Pentagon Officials Faulted for Role in Airplane Manufacturer Scandal"

"Former Fortune 500 CEOs Found Guilty"

"East Coast Communications Company and U.S. Settle for $715 Million"

"Feds Seek $5 Million from Back-Office Veterans"

From Enron to Bernie Madoff, the daily news in print or other media is full of stories of fraud, deceit, money laundering, perjury, and theft. The Olsson Center for Applied Ethics that is part of the Darden School of Business at the University of Virginia has created a Business Ethics timeline showing major ethical events over the past few years. Some of the names are familiar—Enron, WorldCom, Adelphia, Tyco, Bristol-Myers, Freddie Mac, AIG—and others less so, but all of the cases have resulted in the collapse of companies, heavy fines, and prison sentences for many of the top executives. For more details, see the website at http://dm.darden. virginia.edu/ethicstimeline/.

Where Are the Auditors?

Following the collapse in 2002 of Arthur Andersen, major accounting firm and auditor for Enron, for its conviction for obstruction of justice, the Justice Department turned its attention to the other surviving large accounting firms. Federal regulators began to investigate the "Big Four" firms for possibly setting up tax shelters to assist wealthy clients to evade taxes, thereby cheating both the U.S. government and fellow taxpayers out of billions of dollars. Is protecting the best interests of the client sufficient excuse for manipulating the law? Should the government proceed to indict another major accounting firm on a felony conviction that could result in that company losing its accounting license, or is that punishment outweighed by the potential damage to thousands of the company's clients if the firm goes under? The solution to the existing ethical situation becomes an ethical dilemma of its own.

Corporate Scandals

Enron may have been the first big corporate scandal to come to the public's attention, but it has certainly been followed by numerous others. Familiar names fill the business pages of major newspapers on a daily basis. Accounting firms are held responsible for giving bad (or illegal) advice to their clients. Presidents, CEOs, and CFOs of companies find themselves individually and financially liable for damages. Chief executives face both prison terms and multi-million-dollar fines. Bernie Madoff, creator of the biggest Ponzi scheme ever known, was sentenced to 150 years in prison and a forfeiture of over $17 billion.

According to federal regulators, one family has agreed to turn over 95% of its personal assets, totaling over $1.2 billion dollars, to its privately owned corporation to pay back the government and victims of a long-running fraud. The following fictional case study is based on that case.

case study	**Case Study #1—The Mighty Have Fallen**

Mr. X, son of Italian immigrants and a pioneer in cable television, was a hero to his hometown where he built his communications company into a corporate giant. Over the years, however, a combination of unwise business decisions, over-expansion, and extravagant personal spending led to his company's downfall. Although some people have labeled Mr. X the worst example of a CEO of the corporate scandal era for stealing from the resources of his company, others say the blame also extends to the lenders, auditors, lawyers, and analysts who should have been acting to protect the best interests of the public. A combination of commercial banks loaned Mr. X's company over $3 billion to be repaid by the company and Mr. X's family. Later, when the company securities lost value and the excessive personal spending of members of the family mounted, the company collapsed, filing for bankruptcy and wiping out all of the public stockholders.

The highly recognized corporate auditor of Mr. X's company had recommended that the rarely seen co-borrowing of family and company be disclosed, but that was never done. The corporation's board of directors actually approved the loans, and even the Securities and Exchange Commission (SEC) was apparently aware of the unusual arrangement. The whistle was eventually blown when a bond analyst was not satisfied with evasive answers given when company officials were questioned about the amount of existing corporate debt.

In one respect, Mr. X's family differed from other corporate tycoons in that they never sold any of their stock in the company, perhaps always believing that things would eventually turn around in their favor. Back in Mr. X's hometown, the family is still praised for the good works they provided to the town, even by some of those financially hurt by the company's fall.

For Discussion

1. Should family members be held personally responsible for corporate debt?

2. Is it the responsibility of the accounting firm's auditor to report unusual debt arrangements to an outside source?

3. Are there others who have shared in the financial responsibility to shareholders of Mr. X's company?

4. Why would people in Mr. X's hometown still believe in and support the family?

The greatest tragedy of the corporate scandals is the devastating impact on individuals and families who lose their life savings due to the unethical and fraudulent behavior of others. Even with the large settlements made by an indicted company, the little guys at the bottom of the pyramid are lucky to receive anything back on their investment. Sending the white-collar perpetrators to prison might provide some sense of satisfaction, but it does little to restore the consumer's confidence in large corporations, stock brokerages, and accounting firms.

For more specific up-to-date information on corporate scandals, see the Institute for Global Ethics website at www.globalethics.org.

True/False Questions (Circle the correct answer)

1.   T   F   Accounting firm XYZ was *NOT* justified in testifying in its defense that it acted only to protect the best interests of its client.

2.   T   F   Professor Q was correct in teaching his students that ethics and morality are *ALWAYS* defined by philosophers as meaning the same thing.

2. Learning Objective: Outline specific guidelines for ethical business practice and give examples of professional associations that provide a code of ethics for their members.

■ Corporate Code of Ethics

Business corporations today are all encouraged to develop a written code of ethics. The very act of sitting down to prepare such a code has proven to be extremely helpful in raising a sense of awareness of the importance of ethical business behavior. A list of companies with a corporate code of ethics includes many familiar names: AT&T, Burger King, Campbell Soup, Coca-Cola, Costco, FedEx, Hewlett-Packard, Honda of America, IBM, John Deere, Johnson & Johnson, Kraft Foods, Lockheed Martin, Lowes, Motorola, NIKE, Pepsi, RE/MAX, Sara Lee, Schweppes, Shell, Texas Instruments, Verizon, Weyerhaeuser, and Williams-Sonoma. In our current hi-tech world we also see Amazon, Apple, Dell, Facebook, Google, Intel, Netflix, LinkedIn, Microsoft, Twitter, and Yahoo with a written Code of Ethics. And if you are looking to write a Code of Ethics for your business, there is even a website that will help you—see Business-in-a-Box.com. You must remember, however, that the most perfectly written Code of Ethics will make little difference in the day-to-day operations of the business unless everyone affiliated with the company from the President or CEO down to the file clerk not only reads it, but is given time to discuss the issues involved and to see the Code in action on a daily basis.

Guidelines for Ethical Business

The George S. May International Company provided consulting services to businesses in a wide variety of categories for over 85 years, serving more than 500,000 clients in over 3,000 different industries. After May's death in 1962, the company continued successfully under varied leadership for many years. Unfortunately, after a series of upper management problems, the company was closed in 2011. Although written many years ago, the original George May "Guidelines for Ethical Business Operations" continue to provide a sound basis for ethical business practice. See Figure 1.1.

Figure 1.1 | Guidelines for Ethical Business Operations

Laws—Laws are created to help society function. Is the action you are considering legal? Do you know the laws governing the activity? In general, ignorance of a law is no excuse for breaking the law.

Rules and Procedures—Companies create specific policies and procedures to help the business function appropriately. Typically, these rules have developed as ways to keep the company successful and avoid problems. How does your planned action compare to what is stated in the company's policies and procedures?

Values—These social principles help to create society's laws and a company's policies and procedures. In turn, laws and policies reinforce the values. One example of values in operation is to ask yourself: "Does the action I'm considering follow not only the letter of the law, but also the 'spirit' of the law?" Is your action in agreement with the overall purpose of a law or rule? Or are you attempting to find a loophole?

Conscience—This internal sense of right and wrong develops from an early age. Your conscience recognizes certain principles that lead to feelings of guilt if you violate the principles. Will your actions make you feel guilty? Can you truly justify your actions?

Promises—Business is based upon trust. It is the belief that what is stated will be delivered. Will your action live up to the commitment that you made to the other person (customer, client, supplier, employee, employer) in the business relationship? Will your action build more trust?

Heroes—Every person has at least one individual who is a role model in some way. A hero may be a parent, teacher, coach, mentor, or friend. Is your action what your hero would do in the same situation? How would your hero act?

Source: George S. May International Company.

As you read the guidelines carefully, ask yourself how these may be applied to your own practice of real estate.

The first guideline is **Laws**. We have local, state, and national laws that affect our real estate business. Every state requires that real estate professionals be licensed and complete a specified number of hours of continuing education for relicensure. Most states have laws requiring disclosure to the consumer of agency relationships, property condition, and environmental issues. There are federal laws governing areas of communication by way of telephone, email, and faxing.

Next are **Rules and Procedures**. The state licensing authority publishes rules and regulations for obtaining and renewing salesperson or broker licenses, establishment of brokerage offices, handling of escrow funds, and numerous other aspects of operating a real estate business. Local REALTOR® associations have regulations regarding MLS entries and use of lockboxes and keys. Individual companies should have printed policies and procedures regarding agency representation of clients, in addition to procedures to be followed for all listings and sales.

Values and **Conscience** begin at the top. The sense of values and social conscience of the principal broker/owner is usually reflected in the actions of the agents affiliated with that particular office.

Promises are best described by the saying, "Underpromise and overdeliver!" The sure way to gain someone's trust is to promise what you will do—and then do it.

As to **Heroes**, who are yours? Do you try to be like your own personal hero? Do you see yourself as a hero to a new agent in your office, to the young first-time homebuyers you helped find a home, or to the immigrant family of eight who no one else would take the time to assist?

Professional Associations and Companies

Do companies, including real estate brokerage companies, really want to follow these guidelines and strive to perform in an ethical manner at all times? Or is the best description of the marketplace "a place set apart where men may deceive one another," as said by philosopher Anacharsis over 2,500 years ago? Although there is still a good deal of deception going on in our modern-day marketplace, apparently there is also a perceived desire on the part of companies to act honorably and ethically. This is shown in the number of professional organizations and associations that stress the importance of a code of ethics and the development of standards for ethical behavior. A brief sampling of these groups follows:

- The Better Business Bureau (BBB) has promoted fairness and integrity in the marketplace since 1912 with a stated goal to "promote and foster the highest ethical relationship between businesses and the public through voluntary self-regulation, consumer and business education, and service excellence." The BBB website will direct you to your local Better Business Bureau. (www.bbb.org)

- The Ethics and Compliance Officer Association (ECOA) was founded in 1992 and currently has over 1,200 members representing the largest number of ethics and compliance practitioners in the world. (www.theecoa.org)

- Seven set principles make up the code of ethics for the Financial Planning Association (FPA) and are designed to guide members in the practice of professional ethics in the field of financial planning. (www.fpanet.org)

- The Institute of Business Ethics (IBE) believes that companies should always uphold the highest standards of behavior and professional conduct. In addition to stating the IBE's own Code of Ethics on their website, they also provide suggestions for making a code of ethics effective and information on applicable content for a code of ethics company policy. (www.ibe.org.uk)

- In 1978, the Office of Government Ethics (OGE) was established as a result of the Ethics in Government Act. As an agency within the Executive Branch, it acts to prevent and resolve conflict of interest situations occurring with government employees. The most complex changes to the executive branch ethics program in 2013 came as a result of passage of the STOCK Act (Stop Trading on Congressional Knowledge Act of 2012). (www.usoge.gov)

- The Institute for Global Ethics (IGE) is dedicated to promoting ethical behavior in individuals, institutions, and nations through research, public discourse, and practical action. The IGE publishes a free *Ethics Newsline*® that serves as an online source for information on ethics and current events. To subscribe to the Newsline, visit the IGE home page at www.globalethics.org.

- The National Association of REALTORS® (NAR) provided a Code of Ethics for its members as early as 1913. This "living document" is constantly under review and modified to meet the challenge of ongoing changes in the real estate market. The NAR code will be discussed at length in later chapters.

True/False Questions (Circle the correct answer)

1.   T   F   As long as a company has a published code of ethics, there will *NEVER* be a problem of unethical behavior on the part of its employees.

2.   T   F   The requirement that ethics be included in the business school curriculum was initiated by the Institute for Global Ethics.

3. Learning Objective: Describe ethical issues that exist in the classroom and in the sports world and how they are being addressed.

■ Ethics and the Classroom

Mark Twain tells us that no man is born with morals. He is also credited with saying that, "It is noble to be good, and it's nobler to teach others to be good—and less trouble!" This leads us to the position of ethics in the academic environment of today.

Ethics is an important classroom issue at many levels: course curriculum, instructor choices, and student behavior.

Business Ethics Courses

Courses in business ethics are becoming more popular and are often required on college campuses throughout the country. Following in the wake of corporate scandals, business schools in particular are recognizing the need to instill ethical standards and a basis for ethical behavior in today's students. In a study conducted by the Aspen Institute in 2003, MBA students in the United States, Canada, and Britain expressed their concerns that their schools were not doing enough to prepare them for the ethical dilemmas they might face in the business world.

Changes began early at the Akron College of Business Administration, the Prudential Business Ethics Center at Rutgers, the Fisher College of Business at Ohio State, the Kellogg School of Management at Northwestern University, the Katz School of Management at the University of Pittsburgh, and the Haas School of Business at the University of California-Berkeley. According to the Aspen Institute, between 2001 and 2011 the percentage of schools requiring courses dedicated to social, ethical, and environmental issues went from 34% in 2001 to 79% in 2011. By 2011, the Aspen Top 10 list was headed by the business schools at Stanford, Notre Dame, Yale, Northwestern, and University of Michigan. Harvard Business School did not participate in the Aspen study but has been actively involved in ethics training since the 1980s. Likewise, the Stern School of Business at NYU claims to have required a course in ethics for the past 30 years.

One concern is that this revived interest in the study of ethics that has come about as a result of recent corporate scandals will fade over time. Schools continually face the pressure to expand their curricula to include topics that are focused on technology, the internet, globalization, and the environment to the point that there is a concern that the study of business ethics may once again become neglected.

The Association to Advance Collegiate Schools of Business (AACSB) that accredits business schools now requires that ethics be included in the course curriculum. In 2013, the AACSB completed a major revision to their accreditation standards. The new standards place a greater emphasis on social responsibility and ethics. An interesting sidelight has been the use of convicted (and now released) felons to weave more ethics training into the classroom. The following case study is based on a real-life couple.

| case study | **Case Study #2—The Duo of Deceit** |

For Discussion

John Q had a busy and successful career as a municipal attorney, trial lawyer, law school professor, and former business partner of a well-known football star. It all came to an end, however, when he and his wife were arrested, tried, and convicted on 19 counts of fraud and tax evasion. Prosecutors in their 1999 trial brought out incidences of tax evasion, consorting with mobsters, and looting their children's trust funds. Mr. Q served five years in federal prison and his wife served four. Known as the "duo of deceit," they had lived by the mantra, "Everybody does it." Finding legal loopholes to justify their actions had become a way of life for them. Today, they have started a new career giving lectures at business schools on how to avoid going astray as they did. In their seminars, the couple now stresses the importance of not letting success inflate your ego, choosing your partners wisely, and listening to your own conscience.

1. Does wealth in and of itself lead to unethical behavior?

2. Are students more, or less, apt to listen to the advice of convicted felons?

3. Despite accusations of many types of corrupt behavior, what was the couple ultimately convicted of and sent to prison for?

4. Does support of John Q's new teaching career imply forgiveness or condoning of his former bad behavior?

Cheating

An even more immediate problem in colleges and universities today is that of cheating. An extraordinarily high percentage of students admit to having cheated on exams during their college years. An even greater problem is that of students pirating information from the internet and presenting it as their own work. In some cases, entire thesis papers have been downloaded and submitted. The problem is so large that there are actually websites designed to monitor students' papers and to catch such offenders. Turnitin is an internet-based service that can be purchased by schools and universities that is designed to prevent plagiarism by the students. In some cases, a teacher may find that an entire assignment has been "lifted" from the internet. In others, only selected sections of the paper have been copied. Often, the problem is just the lack of proper citation of the originator of the information. Working with the system, the teacher and student can often work out the problem satisfactorily whereas in the past, the student would have just received a failing grade.

The internet is a fantastic source for research on any subject and can make the scholar's task much easier. The downside is that there is so much incorrect information appearing on the internet today that it just gets perpetuated from one article or blog to another. Good research requires careful attention to the actual source and verification of the information given. Gone are the days of searching out volumes in the library, laboriously writing out notes, and then spending long hours compiling that information into a term paper or a master's or doctoral thesis. Fewer hours spent in front of a computer in the comforts of home or dorm are certainly preferable but are not intended to provide the student with an easy way out. One professor at a small business school told of a student who was unable to defend his master's thesis at the oral jury presentation because he didn't really understand what some of the words meant!

In other cases, professors are bribed to raise a grade or turn a blind eye to classroom cheating just to keep a particular student in school because the parents are major contributors to the athletic or alumni fund. In one case, it was actually the *ethics* professor who was involved!

Future Outlook

There are some encouraging changes with regard to ethics in the academic world. A few colleges have actually dropped athletic programs in favor of more concentration on scholastic achievement. Colleges and universities are developing stricter policies to circumvent internet pirating. Hopefully, the trend toward more required courses in business ethics will diminish the number of corporate fraud cases that have been seen in recent days. Unfortunately, there is always a chance that Mason Cooley was right when he wrote in *City Aphorisms*, New York, 1988, "Reading about ethics is as likely to improve one's behavior as reading about sports is to make one into an athlete."

■ Ethics and the Locker Room

The shadow of steroids and other performance-enhancing drugs hangs over all aspects of the sports arena today. Famous sports heroes are paraded through congressional hearings; gold medals are revoked and awarded to the runners-up; and competitions are plagued with drug testing—all because some athletes are so determined to win that they will do anything to increase their physical status and power.

It broke many people's hearts when Olympic gold medalist Marion Jones admitted to using performance-enhancing drugs in 2007. She lost her medals for track-and-field events and was sent to prison for six months for lying to investigators. Today, she shares her story with young athletes in hopes that they will choose to avoid taking the drugs.

Possibly the most notorious of the athletes caught up in a doping scandal is Lance Armstrong. Armstrong won seven Tour de France titles in cycling along with many other medals. As a cancer survivor, he gained the admiration and respect of millions of people. When accused of taking performance-enhancing drugs, he denied their use, and fought hard to defend his position for many years. When he ultimately confessed to using the drugs, maintaining a defense of "everybody does it," it rocked not just the cycling world but all those who had believed in him and supported him. The USADA (United States Anti-Doping Agency) stripped him of his medals and banned him from cycling. He resigned as chairman of the Lance Armstrong Foundation (now the Livestrong Foundation), a supporting group for cancer victims which he had founded in 1997.

Many Major League Baseball stars have been caught up in the use of steroids scandals in recent years. Some of the most well-known are Roger Clemens, Barry Bonds, Mark McGwire, and most recently, Alex Rodriguez (A-Rod). In July, the League was considering banning Rodriguez from baseball for life. Ultimately, the decision was to ban him from the 2014 season. You have to wonder: was it worth it? Clemens and Bonds were recently made aware of the long-reaching effects of these accusations. Despite being two of the biggest names in baseball history, they were both rejected in the current year's voting for the National Baseball Hall of Fame.

Promising high school athletes are wooed by major universities with scholarships, new cars, and allowances to ensure that the school gain or retain high standings in the athletic world. This has been a common practice for many years but also raises some ethical questions. Is it fair for these athletes to receive special treatment like upgraded dorm facilities, higher-quality meals, and weekly allowances? Should the star football players be excused from classes on Fridays in order to rest up for Saturday's game? Is it really okay for a professor to move a grade from D+ to C- just to maintain a basketball player's eligibility?

case study	**Case Study #3—Is Winning Everything?**

A TV news magazine told the story of a small New England prep school that had enjoyed a good reputation for graduating well-behaved, knowledgeable young men into the community for over 100 years. Unfortunately, school enrollment was dropping and the school was about to go under. The decision was made to bring in outstanding young basketball stars from all over the country (on scholarships, of course) to build a team that would win honors and trophies, generating new exposure for the school, increased enrollment, and greater financial support. It worked. The school is back in a strong financial position; more young men are achieving a good academic education; and the basketball team continues to win games. Is there an ethical problem here?

For Discussion

Relating the basic concept of this story to a real estate office, answer the following questions:

1. Would it be right for broker W to pay for top-of-the-line laptop computers, PDAs, and camera cell phones for four new agents that he believed would raise the level of professionalism (and bring in more business) for his office?

2. Would the other agents in broker W's office be justified in complaining that this was an unfair decision?

3. If more business is generated for the office, will everyone benefit?

4. What would be a better way to achieve broker W's desired result?

True/False Questions (Circle the correct answer)

1.   T   F   There is no guarantee that the emphasis given today on including business ethics in the approved curriculum will continue into the future.

2.   T   F   Maria forgot that she has a six-page report due tomorrow on the impact brown fields have on city development. Her *BEST* solution is to research the internet for an article on that topic, copy it, and turn it in on time.

■ Conclusion

Would merely having a corporate code of ethics have prevented a major business tycoon from stealing money from the corporation's accounts? Does signing a pledge at the end of a master's thesis guarantee that the student has not copied material directly from the internet? Does pledging to follow the Code of Ethics mean that every REALTOR® will always protect the best interests of a client? Obviously, the answer is no in all cases. Neither written rules and regulations nor a published code of ethics will ever be able to ensure ethical behavior on the part of all individuals. The written word can, however, provide a place to start.

Whether in the boardroom, the classroom, the locker room, or the real estate salesroom, time devoted to honest discussion of ethical principles can make a difference. Reviewing a case study based on an actual experience gives people an opportunity to examine different aspects of a situation without it becoming a personal issue. There is often more than one answer to an ethical question. Hearing and discussing different sides of these hypothetical case studies might be helpful the next time a person faces a similar ethical dilemma.

The exposure of misdealing at the corporate level, the emphasis on required business ethics courses for tomorrow's chief executives, the requirement for more ethics training for real estate professionals—all of these efforts will hopefully lead to higher standards of ethical behavior in today's world and that of tomorrow.

■ Review Questions

1. Situational ethics can be *BEST* described as ethics based on
   a. the early teachings of Socrates.
   b. always doing the right thing.
   c. behavior determined by circumstances.
   d. congressional rulings.

2. The greatest tragedy resulting from the corporate scandals is the
   a. bad publicity for formerly admired companies.
   b. exposure of lack of ethics in the business world.
   c. impact on individuals losing their life savings.
   d. former CEOs and CFOs sent to jail.

3. All of the following statements regarding ethics and law are true *EXCEPT*
   a. ethics and law are not synonymous.
   b. ethical behavior cannot be legislated.
   c. ethics never go beyond the limitations of the law.
   d. the law draws a firm black and white line between right and wrong.

4. After the collapse of Arthur Andersen, the government began to investigate the remaining "Big Four" accounting firms for
   a. obstruction of justice.
   b. filing erroneous tax forms.
   c. setting up tax shelters to assist clients evading taxes.
   d. cheating their clients.

5. The primary reason for the collapse of the Arthur Andersen accounting and auditing firm was
   a. the lack of response to the Securities and Exchange Commission.
   b. a felony indictment against the CEO of the firm.
   c. giving advice to a major client that led to tax evasion and fraud.
   d. overspending by the board of directors.

6. The *MOST* important element of developing a corporate Code of Ethics is the
   a. way the code is written.
   b. act of sitting down to prepare a code.
   c. number of articles in the code.
   d. number of people preparing the code.

7. Of the six practical guidelines for ethical business behavior outlined in May's "Guidelines for Ethical Business Operations," the ones *MOST* likely to result from the "top down" are
   a. Laws.
   b. Rules and Procedures.
   c. Values and Conscience.
   d. Promises and Heroes.

8. George May's first guideline for ethical business concerns laws. In the real estate business, this can be seen in all of the following *EXCEPT*
   a. state licensure law.
   b. federal and state fair housing law.
   c. MLS and lockbox procedures.
   d. mandatory disclosure of environmental hazards.

9. The "hero" in a real estate office would *MOST* likely be the agent who
   a. made the most sales for the year.
   b. had the highest number of listings.
   c. was willing to work with low-income renters.
   d. provided a Christmas party for all agents.

10. The first organization to promote fairness and integrity in the market place was the
    a. Better Business Bureau.
    b. Ethics and Compliance Officer Association.
    c. Institute of Business Ethics.
    d. Office of Government Ethics.

11. A dean of a small college is apt to run into ethical questions in all of the following situations *EXCEPT* the
    a. behavior of individual students.
    b. selection of course curriculum.
    c. decisions made by professors.
    d. calculation of grade point averages.

12. The revived interest in the study of ethics in business schools came about due to the
    a. overall changes in curriculum prevalent today.
    b. drug scandals in the sports world.
    c. large number of corporate scandals that have occurred.
    d. increased amount of plagiarism.

13. Cheating has always occurred in universities, but today's biggest problem is
    a. one student taking an exam for another.
    b. bribing the professor for a higher grade.
    c. claiming information taken from the internet as original work.
    d. professor ignoring cheating in the classroom.

14. The sports scandals that have received the *MOST* attention are those concerned with
    a. deliberately injuring another competitor.
    b. placing bets either for or against one's own team.
    c. the use of steroids and other performance-enhancing drugs.
    d. bribing officials.

15. Many athletes have been punished for unethical behavior over the past few years. Who was forced to give back at least seven major medals?
    a. Alex Rodriguez
    b. Lance Armstrong
    c. Marion Jones
    d. Barry Bonds

2 Ethics and the Real Estate Professional

Learning Objectives

Upon completion of this chapter, you will be able to

- discuss the role of professional organizations and state regulators in protecting the rights of clients and customers involved in real estate transactions;

- provide examples of the obligations and responsibilities of residential and commercial agents as buyer agent, seller agent, dual agent, or designated agent, including property managers and leasing agents; and

- identify potential ethical issues facing appraisers, settlement attorneys/title company agents, and lenders.

■ Key Terms

Appraisal Institute	designated agent	Mortgage Bankers
ARELLO	dual agent	Association
Association of Mortgage	FSBO	National Association of
Brokers	Megan's Law	REALTORS®
buyer agent		

■ Introduction

Although there is a growing interest in real estate being offered as a degree option in many colleges and universities, most of today's real estate professionals still enter the business from some other line of work. Some come from the business world; others may have been teachers or members of the medical profession. Frequently, those involved in the financing side of real estate decide to try it from the sales viewpoint. In some parts of the country, there are always military or government retirees preparing for a second career. And, of course, real estate is an attractive option for those presently working in some other form of sales. Regardless of the backgrounds, whether business, academic, sales, or any other field, lessons learned from past experiences will inevitably be carried into the real estate profession.

1. Learning Objective: Discuss the role of professional organizations and state regulators in protecting the rights of clients and customers involved in real estate transactions.

■ The Need for Ethical Behavior

For most homeowners, the home represents their greatest financial asset. It becomes obvious, then, that ethical behavior and a code of standards for ethical business practices have a great significance for those involved in the practice of real estate. The real estate broker, the appraiser, the lender, and the settlement agent are all dealing with not only the largest financial investment the consumer will ever make but also with the potential homeowner's hopes and dreams of a better way of life and permanent status within the community.

Professional Associations

Recognizing the importance of being able to assure the public that they will be treated ethically in their real estate transactions, all of the real estate–related professional organizations require their members to subscribe to a code of ethics. Examples are the

- National Association of REALTORS® Code of Ethics,
- Appraisal Institute Code of Professional Ethics and Standards of Professional Appraisal Practice, and
- Mortgage Bankers Association Canons of Ethics.

One of the primary goals of these professional associations is to increase the public's awareness of the values and integrity that can be expected from dealing with real estate professionals who are members of that organization. The National Association of REALTORS® has conducted an extensive TV advertising campaign for several years that dramatizes the benefits of working with a REALTOR® who subscribes to a code of ethics.

State Regulators

All 50 states, the District of Columbia, and all Canadian provinces require real estate practitioners to be licensed. However, a licensed agent is not *required* to join one of the professional associations where the agent would be subject to a mandatory code of ethics. Membership in a professional organization is by choice. In some states, the official Rules and Regulations for Licensees includes a section on Standards of Conduct. These Standards of Conduct are usually very similar to the subjects covered under the professional association's code. Many states have now

mandated ethics education for their licensees. In most states, three or four hours of ethics training is required or is acceptable as an elective for continuing education credits. The Association of Real Estate License Law Officials (ARELLO) promotes uniform standards for administering and enforcing state license laws. ARELLO guidelines are significant in the preparation of all real estate prelicensing and continuing education courses, including those on the subject of ethics.

Customer and Client Relationships

The original organization that ultimately became the National Association of REALTORS® (NAR) was formed in 1908 by a group of responsible real estate brokers striving to develop higher ethical standards for those practicing real estate in this country. The first Code of Ethics was developed in 1913. In 1924, pledging to subscribe to the Code of Ethics became a requirement of membership. That mandate continues to apply to the over one million members of the NAR today. For over five decades, the code made the question of, "Who do you represent?" very clear. All agents, whether listing or selling, involved in the transaction had a fiduciary responsibility to the seller. When surveys of both sellers and buyers taken in the late 1970s showed that most consumers *assumed* that the selling agent was actually working on behalf of the buyer—not the seller—concern was raised about undisclosed dual agency, fraud, and possible rescission of contracts.

By the late 1980s, legislation was passed by most state legislatures requiring that disclosure of agency relationship be made to all potential buyers. Buyers had to acknowledge that they were customers and that the agent was primarily responsible for promoting the best interests of the seller. If the buyer wanted to be represented by the agent, a separate agreement had to be signed.

Throughout the 1990s, the demand for true representation for the buyer began to grow. The buying public wanted to know that the agent with whom they were working was in fact representing their best interests. Buyer agency became the buzzword, and states started to formulate agency law as it applied to real estate transactions. By the mid-1990s, revisions appeared in the NAR Code of Ethics reflecting this change. Stated definitions of *client* and *customer* were added. No longer did submission to an MLS system automatically create an agency relationship with the seller, nor did payment of a commission. The agent representing the buyer could now be paid through the transaction (i.e., seller to listing broker, listing broker to selling broker, selling broker to the buyer agent). These changes in license law and in the NAR Code of Ethics made it possible for the agent to now act as the true representative of the buyer. This may have cleared up the question, "Who do I work for?" but resulted in even more possible conflict of interest issues.

True/False Questions (Circle the correct answer)

1.   T   F   The only reason that ethical business practice is important for real estate professionals is that they are dealing with the largest investment most people will ever make.

2.   T   F   The primary responsibility of ARELLO is to provide a Standards of Conduct to be used in all states.

2. Learning Objective: Provide examples of the obligations and responsibilities of residential and commercial agents as buyer agent, seller agent, dual agent, or designated agent, including property managers and leasing agents.

■ Agency Issues for Residential Agents

Building on legislation passed in the 1980s, state agency laws began to further define the relationship between an agent and a purchaser or an agent and a seller. A client is the one with whom the agent has established a brokerage relationship, which must be in writing in order to be enforceable. (In some places, an oral agreement is legal but cannot be legally enforced.) The other party to the transaction is a customer, who must be treated honestly but is not legally represented by the agent. The duties and responsibilities of the agent are determined by state law and are expressed in the agreement.

The Agreement

Both listing agreements and buyer agency agreements are actually a contract between the consumer client and the broker (not the salesperson). A question of conflict of interest may arise when two agents from the same brokerage firm have competing contracts for a property listed by the company with which they are both affiliated. The written buyer agency agreement should make it clear that other agents from the same brokerage firm may have other clients interested in any of the firm's listings.

Designated Agent

In order to avoid a potential conflict of interest when both the listing agent and the selling (buyer) agent are from the same firm, some states now provide for an agency status called *designated agent* where one agent represents the seller and the other agent represents the buyer. The designated agent for the seller is fully responsible for protecting the best interests of the seller client. The designated agent for the buyer is fully responsible for protecting the best interests of the buyer. In this case, the broker still has a responsibility to both seller and buyer and is acting as a *dual agent*.

Dual Agent

Dual agency occurs when an agent (broker) represents both buyer and seller in the same transaction. In effect, the agent now has two clients and has equal fiduciary or statutory responsibility to both. In states that do not recognize designated agents, dual agency occurs when one agent from a company represents a buyer who wishes to purchase one of that company's listings. In some states, dual agency is not allowed. In others, it is allowed but with limitations. For example, in Maryland, dual agency is allowed with one exception: a listing agent may not sell his own listing as a dual agent. The listing agent must remain as the representative of the seller with the purchaser treated as a customer, or another agent from the same company can step in to represent the buyer.

Disclosure

In all cases, full disclosure of the dual agency relationship must be made with all parties to the transaction giving written consent. This becomes disclosed dual agency. To avoid any potential conflict of interest, some brokerage firms mandate that a listing agent always work solely as the seller's agent. This would seem to simplify matters, but in some situations, this might not be true. Even though the legal aspects of a situation are very clear-cut, an ethical dilemma might occur when circumstances go beyond the limits of the law. One example involves the listing agent's responsibility with regard to Megan's Law. *Megan's Law* is the familiar name for federal legislation requiring that released sex offenders be registered with their local law enforcement agency, which is responsible for making that information available to all citizens. Every state is responsible for determining how this information is to be distributed. The listing agent may be presented with an ethical dilemma over how to handle the implications of this law.

Limited Representative

Some states have now included a category of "Limited Representative" under their agency law. A limited representative must make full disclosure of exactly which duties of agency will be performed and which ones will not.

■ Understanding Ethical Dilemmas Through Case Studies

The case studies that follow are all based on real-life situations. Names and circumstances have been changed to protect the innocent and, sometimes, the not so innocent. Part I explores situations creating ethical questions for residential agents. Each case study is followed by "For Discussion" questions and multiple-choice questions relating to the case. Ethical dilemmas that occur in other real estate specialty areas will be featured in Part II. No final resolutions are given. The cases are left open for individual or group decision as to whether an ethics violation has occurred. Answers to the multiple-choice questions are given in the Answer Key that follows Chapter 6.

Part I—Residential Agents

case study	Case Study #1—Multiple Clients

Martin has shown his buyer client Sally at least ten properties for sale over the past two months. Sally actually made less-than-full-price offers on three of the properties but lost out to better offers. Yesterday, Martin showed Sally a new listing on Orchard Street that had just been listed by Jim, one of Martin's fellow agents at XYZ Realty. Sally wanted to think it over and said she would get back to Martin today.

Early this morning, while Martin was on desk duty, George walked into the office. He had seen the For Sale sign on the Orchard Street property and wanted to see it right away. Martin quickly went over the Buyer Agency Agreement with George, obtained George's signature, and proceeded to show the house. George loved it and returned to the office with Martin to prepare an Offer to Purchase. The contract was written at full price with a contingency for a home inspection and settlement in 30 days.

Luckily for Martin, listing agent Jim was in the office and arranged to meet the seller over her lunch break. Seller Helen had just been informed by her boss that morning that she was to be promoted and transferred to the new branch office in another city in 30 days, rather than the three months that she had thought was the case. Helen signed the contract, agreeing to the home inspection contingency and a settlement date in 30 days.

At 4:00 PM, Sally left a message for Martin that she wanted to meet him at 7:00 PM to write up an offer on the Orchard Street house. When Martin called back and told her that a contract had just been ratified on the property, she was very disappointed. When Sally found out after further inquiry that Martin was actually the selling agent on the Orchard Street property, she was furious. She accused him of failing in his agency responsibility to her as her buyer agent. She felt that he had not acted in her best interests because he knew that she was interested in purchasing that property, and she told him that she planned to charge him with an ethics violation and to sue the brokerage firm for violating state agency law.

For Discussion

1. Was Martin promoting and protecting Sally's best interests?

2. Was Martin promoting and protecting George's best interests?

3. Is it possible to promote and protect the best interests of two clients when they are interested in the same property?

4. Should Martin have called Sally to tell her George was writing an offer?

5. Would it have made any difference if the property were listed with another company?

6. Does the broker have a responsibility to Sally? To George? To Helen?

Case Study Questions

1. All of the following statements of facts involved in this case are true and would have an impact on the ethical situation *EXCEPT*
   a. Sally has made offers on three properties.
   b. Sally told Martin she might want to buy the Orchard Street property.
   c. Martin brought the Orchard Street property to George's attention.
   d. Sally feels that Martin has failed his agency responsibility to her.

2. In this situation, the broker at XYZ Realty has a primary duty to promote and protect the best interest of
   a. Sally.
   b. George.
   c. Helen.
   d. all three clients.

case study   **Case Study #2—For Sale by Owner (FSBO)**

Marcia has a signed buyer agency agreement with Judy. After three months, they have still not been able to find a property in Judy's price range that meets her particular needs. Judy suffers from multiple sclerosis and is frequently confined to a wheelchair. Twice they thought they had found a condominium unit that would be acceptable, but in both cases, the property was gone before they could write up an offer. Yesterday, one of Judy's co-workers told her that a couple who lived on the ground floor of her building was planning to move. The Gonzalezes had mentioned they would now need to move because they had just had twins and needed more space. She also knew that the Gonzalezes planned to sell the property themselves in order to save paying a commission. They had very little cash to put down on a town house they wished to buy. Judy called Marcia, who then called the Gonzalezes to see if they would allow her to show the property and if they would consider paying her a buyer agent commission. They agreed to let Marcia show Judy the unit but would not agree to pay any commission. Marcia took Judy over to see the unit today and noted that although the unit was on the first floor, there were two steps leading up to the front door of the building. She also pointed out that the front windows of the unit opened directly onto the street and the bedroom window was behind dense shrubbery.

For Discussion

1. Was Marcia acting in Judy's best interest by showing the FSBO unit?

2. Was Marcia acting in Judy's best interest by pointing out the possible hazard of easily accessible windows for a ground floor unit, or was she trying to discourage her from buying it?

3. Should Marcia expect Judy to pay her buyer agent's commission?

4. Should Marcia have told Judy to look at the property by herself?

5. Should Marcia have tried to further negotiate with the Gonzalezes by raising the asking price to include enough for a commission?

6. If the Gonzalezes agreed to raise the price and pay a commission, could Marcia have rebated a part of the commission to Judy?

Case Study Questions

1. As Judy's buyer agent, Marcia should
   a. show only properties listed on the local MLS.
   b. ask the Gonzalezes to sign a listing agreement.
   c. discourage Judy from working with a FSBO.
   d. do her best to help Judy obtain the property she wants.

2. Marcia's *BEST* approach to the Gonzalezes is to
   a. ask them to sign a listing agreement with her.
   b. tell them she will only show the property after they agree to pay her a commission.
   c. make the contract contingent on the Gonzalezes paying her commission.
   d. discuss optional ways that a commission could be included in the sales price.

case study	## Case Study #3—Selling Your Own Listing

Tony has a new listing in a very sought-after neighborhood. When he held an open house on Sunday, at least 20 people came through. Mr. and Mrs. Lee spent almost an hour looking through the house and decided that it met all of their needs. They asked Tony what they needed to do in order to purchase the property. Tony explained that he obviously had a broker/client relationship with the seller but that he would be happy to write up an offer on their behalf. He explained that with their permission, he could be a disclosed dual agent and would represent both the Lees and the seller. Mr. Lee was not too happy with this arrangement, but Mrs. Lee had her heart set on buying the house, and so he agreed. When Tony met with seller Julia later that evening to present the contract, she was dismayed to learn that Tony was now also acting on behalf of the buyers. The offer was $10,000 less than what she wanted, but she did agree to sign the contract, accepting the dual agency position.

Five days later, when the Lees completed their home inspection, they came back with a list of five items that they wanted repaired prior to settlement. When Tony brought Julia the form stating that the home inspection contingency would be removed as long as the five items listed were taken care of prior to settlement, she accused him of not protecting her best interests. She said he was not acting in her best interest when he allowed the home inspector to pry behind drywall in the basement (disclosing a small leak) and to pull up carpet in the dining room (revealing old pet stains). Also, the inspector had suggested that several large old trees in the backyard should be at least trimmed, if not removed, to prevent possible storm damage to the house. Furthermore, she felt that Tony had urged her to accept a contract for less than the asking price which she and Tony had agreed on at the time the house was listed.

Tony returned to the Lees to explain that the seller had reluctantly agreed to take care of four of the five items listed on the contingency form but that the work suggested for the trees was not really an integral part of the working systems of the house and that the seller refused to take any action. The Lees now felt that they should have had their own agent who would have better protected their interests. After all, anyone could see that if one of those trees fell, it would severely damage the roof of the house.

For Discussion

1. Was Tony representing the seller's best interests?
2. Was Tony representing the buyers' best interests?
3. How else could Tony have handled the sale?
4. Could Tony have influenced the home inspector?

Case Study Questions

1. When the Lees expressed interest in purchasing Tony's listing, he should have
   a. written the contract without discussing agency.
   b. discussed the alternative of bringing in another agent to represent them.
   c. signed them up as buyer clients.
   d. refused to work with them due to a conflict of interest.

2. The biggest problem that occurred relative to the removal of the home inspection contingency was that
   a. there were too many items listed for repair.
   b. the inspector pulled up some carpet.
   c. the trees were not part of the physical condition of the house.
   d. neither the buyer nor the seller felt that Tony represented their best interests.

| case study | **Case Study #4—Megan's Law** |

Gloria met with Mr. and Mrs. Martinez to list their three-bedroom, split-level home in a popular neighborhood for people with young children due to the proximity of both an elementary school and a public park. In the course of the conversation with the Martinezes about their future plans, Gloria learned that the reason they wished to move is that they had learned that the 45-year-old son of an elderly couple who lived on their block had just been released from a 15-year prison sentence as a sex offender and was returning to the neighborhood to live with his parents. The Martinezes did not want to live so close to this person because they have two sons, ages 5 and 7.

Because this is not a physical feature of the house, there is no requirement in Gloria's state for such a disclosure to be made. Gloria listed the home at a reasonable price and anticipated that it should be a quick sale, hopefully to someone with their own buyer agent.

The next day, Gloria received a call from Jack and Susan. Jack was being transferred to this city in three weeks, and they were in town for the weekend to look at property. They saw the For Sale sign and wanted to see the house immediately. Gloria met them at the house and they loved it. When they wanted to prepare an offer right there at the kitchen table, she explained that she worked for the seller and would not actually be representing them. Having bought and sold many homes in the past, they didn't care about representation—they just wanted to buy this house. In the process of writing up the offer, Gloria learned that they have six-year-old twin girls and are expecting another child in six months.

Gloria is now faced with an ethical dilemma: should she tell them about the neighbor and risk losing the sale for her client, or should she remain silent and risk the guilt if something should happen to one of the children?

For Discussion

1. Is Gloria obligated to tell Jack and Susan about the neighbor?
2. Would Gloria be violating her responsibility to Mr. and Mrs. Martinez if she discloses something that might discourage the buyers?
3. The law says no disclosure is needed. Is that sufficient?
4. How else could Gloria handle this sale?

Case Study Questions

1. When Gloria learned why the Martinez family wished to move, she should have
   a. immediately refused the listing.
   b. pretended she never heard their reason.
   c. discussed the possible need for disclosure with them.
   d. passed the information on to any eventual buyer.

2. If Jack and Susan have concerns about neighborhood issues, they should do any of the following *EXCEPT*
   a. ask the listing agent for all information.
   b. hire their own buyer agent.
   c. check with local law enforcement agency.
   d. canvass the neighborhood.

Part II—Other Real Estate Specialties

Although the state licensing requirements are the same for all real estate practitioners within a state, there are many specialized areas of real estate practice that require extra training and expertise. For this section, the author invited experts in various fields to contribute comments and case studies illustrating the significance of ethics in their daily practice.

Commercial Real Estate Agents

Contributor:

Cindy Chandler, CRE, CCIM, The Chandler Group, Commercial Real Estate Training & Consulting, Charlotte, NC

Real estate professionals specializing in commercial transactions are often members of the National Association of REALTORS® and subscribe to the NAR Code of Ethics. Other commercial professional organizations like Society of Industrial and Office REALTORS® (SIOR), Certified Commercial Investment Member (CCIM), the Counselors of Real Estate (CRE), and REALTORS® Land Institute (RLI) have additional codes of ethics directed to their particular specializations. Institute of Real Estate Management (IREM) has three specific codes of ethics, namely,

- Code of Professional Ethics of the Certified Property Manager,
- Code of Professional Ethics of the Accredited Residential Manager, and
- Minimum Standards and Code of Professional Ethics for the Accredited Management Organization.

Due to the fact that commercial transactions generally take much longer to complete than residential transactions, there is a greater chance for relationships to shift, circumstances to change, and procuring cause to become a muddy issue. The large number of dollars involved in commercial commissions makes them a prime target for less-than-ethical behavior on the part of unscrupulous agents. Problems may also arise when there are multiple players involved in one transaction or when several transactions are involved in one project. In many cases, either the buyer or the seller (or both) wish to maintain total confidentiality. Working with city, county, or state economic development offices adds yet another element to the equation, and local politics frequently plays a strong role.

case study · Case Study #5—How Much Must I Say?

Katherine is the listing agent for a 50-acre residential tract of land that is currently under contract. The buyer is going through the due diligence period and knows that he will have to rezone the property to build zero-lot-line homes as part of a mixed-use project in order to gain city approval.

Across the street from the 50-acre tract is a 200-acre residential tract of lakefront property that has just gone under contract. This property was never openly listed, but Katherine happens to know that Lakeside Development, the buyer, plans to rezone it for a mixed-use project. The plans for this property include high-end homes along the lake, but no decision has been made for the interior portion.

Katherine also knows that Lakeside Development would like to try for higher-density zoning, but based on her own experience, she knows that the city is not likely to approve this request.

Katherine's dilemma is whether or not she needs to disclose to the buyers (who are unrepresented) of her 50-acre piece the potential development coming across the street. These buyers are from out of town and have no real source of information except for Katherine. Although both projects involve residential concepts, the mixed-use concept will eventually add a tremendous amount of housing and commercial construction in an area that has not seen much growth for a number of years. It is possible that knowledge of the potential 200-acre project could affect the financial evaluation of the 50-acre tract by the buyers. Thomas, the agent for the current buyer of that tract, has approached Katherine and asked her to see if the buyer of the 50-acre tract will be willing to collaborate with his buyer in obtaining city approval for the mixed-use rezoning.

To make the situation even more complicated, Katherine is acting as a buyer's agent for Stanley & Co., who has a backup contract on the 200-acre site. Katherine does not want to disclose her buyer-agent status with Stanley & Co. to Thomas, and she is not sure if collaborating on the rezoning process would be in the best interest of her seller client for the 50 acres. It seems that Katherine is the only one who knows all of the players involved and most of the proposed plans. She is concerned about being placed in a position of liability for not disclosing material facts, but she is also concerned about maintaining her responsibility to both her seller client and her buyer client.

For Discussion

1. Does Katherine have any obligation to reveal her knowledge regarding the 200-acre tract to the buyers of the 50-acre tract she has listed?

2. Would Katherine be violating her responsibility to her seller by revealing information that might affect the sale of the 50-acre property?

3. Does the fact that the 200-acre property was never officially on the market affect Katherine's position?

4. Would cooperating with Thomas's idea to collaborate on the rezoning issue affect Katherine's relationship with Stanley & Co.?

5. Should Katherine tell Stanley & Co. about Thomas's offer?

6. Should Katherine tell her seller about Thomas's idea?

Property Managers and Leasing Agents

Contributor:

Frank Burke, Retired owner of Burke & Warren Property Management, Fairfax, VA

State laws vary as to whether property managers and leasing agents must be licensed, but the general rule is that property managers or leasing agents who have the right to sign on behalf of the owner must be licensed.

An ethical situation might arise when multiple applications come in for the same property. The choice of the new tenant must be based solely on financial qualifications. A problem occurs when an owner has specifically told the agent that certain types of applicants are not to be accepted. For example:

■ Owner J refuses to rent to anyone of the Muslim faith.

■ Owner D refuses to rent to families from Korea.

■ Owner W (a Christian minister) refuses to rent to an unmarried couple.

■ Owner M refuses to rent to four single men.

Federal fair housing law prohibits denial of housing based on race, color, religion, national origin, sex, familial status, or mental or physical handicap. The NAR Code of Ethics has added the additional protected classes of sexual orientation and gender identity. State and local jurisdictions may add additional protected classes. Presented with owners such as those listed previously, the leasing agent has no choice either legally or ethically but to refuse, or drop, the rental listing.

When two applications are presented with equal financial qualifications, the safest way is to accept the one that was submitted first. (A time-received date stamp is an important tool for the office.)

There are times when an ethical decision may need to go beyond the strict interpretations of the law.

Case Study #6—The "Get Out of Lease" Card

Jose works for a construction company in Norfolk, Virginia, that specializes in concrete structures. He has been offered a promotion with a substantial increase in pay, provided he agree to fly to Iraq within the next 30 days to join a crew already working on a reconstruction project there. The project is scheduled to last for at least one year. The promotion and the pay increase are attractive to Jose and to his wife, Marianna. However, Marianna is expecting their first child three months from now and wants to return to Miami to be with her parents. Marianna's English is rather poor, and she is frightened to stay alone in the Norfolk area, especially with a baby on the way.

Jose and Marianna are only six months into a one-year lease and have requested that they be allowed to either break the lease or assign it to their friend Carlos who has recently moved to the Norfolk area. Property Manager Angela knows that the law clearly states they cannot arbitrarily break the lease or assign it to someone else. In Virginia, the landlord may refuse to consent to an assignment and does not have to provide any explanation for such action. (In a few states, a landlord may not unreasonably withhold consent to an assignment of lease.)

Angela is sympathetic to Marianna's feelings and would like to help the young couple. She has full authority and responsibility for the leasing of all units.

For Discussion

1. Should Angela just follow the letter of the law and refuse the assignment?

2. Does she have the right to allow the assignment?

3. What action would be in the best interests of the property owners?

Case Study #7—Illegal or Unethical? Or Both?

The majority of Paul's real estate practice is as a buyer agent, but he occasionally works as a leasing/managing agent with tenants. Six months ago, when the Johnsons first came to town, he helped them find a town house to rent. In the lease, he included a provision that in the event they should decide to purchase a home, he would be their buyer agent.

The Johnsons have decided they like the area where they are living but really prefer to be homeowners rather than tenants. They approach Paul to see if their lease could be terminated early so that they can purchase a home in a new subdivision that has just been completed four blocks away from their present town house. Paul reminds them of the provision in their lease that he is to be their buyer agent if they choose to purchase and that they must agree to work with him if they expect to obtain permission for an early termination of the current lease.

For Discussion

1. Would this be an illegal tying arrangement as forbidden by antitrust law?

2. Is Paul acting in the best interests of the town house owner?

3. Is Paul acting in the best interests of the Johnsons?

True/False Questions (Circle the correct answer)

1.   T   F   Prior to the advent of buyer agency, all agents worked to protect the best interests of the seller client and had no responsibility to the purchaser.

2.   T   F   Megan's Law requires real estate agents to provide full disclosure of released (registered) sex offenders who live near a property listed for sale.

3. Learning Objective: Identify potential ethical issues facing appraisers, settlement attorneys/ title company agents, and lenders.

Real Estate Appraisers

Contributor:

Cindi Mariano, ECG Appraisals, Serving the D.C. Metro Area, Alexandria, VA

When the Society of Real Estate Appraisers and the American Institute of Real Estate Appraisers were first formed, they shared a common goal to elevate the profession by establishing high ethics and standards. This goal is carried out today by the Appraisal Institute by making Business Practices and Ethics a required course in continuing education requirements. Some appraisers are also REALTORS® and subscribe to both the REALTOR® Code of Ethics and the Code of Ethics that is part of the Uniform Standards of Professional Appraisal Practice (USPAP). To avoid any possible conflict of interest due to actual or perceived financial gain, REALTORS® who are also appraisers should neither list a property in a neighborhood where they are currently doing an appraisal nor agree to do an appraisal in a neighborhood where they either currently have a listing or know that they will be taking a listing there in the near future. Obviously, there would be a perceived conflict of interest if an appraiser attempted to prepare an appraisal on one of the appraiser's own listings.

For example, Bob lists a house for $250,000 today. Next week, a neighbor asks Bob to appraise her house. This appraisal is now less objective, as Bob might be faced with some bias in performing this appraisal. On the other hand, if Bob was asked to do the appraisal first, without knowledge that the $250,000 house was to become his listing the following week, preset bias would not be a challenge. The conscientious appraiser/REALTOR® will be very careful in these situations.

Appraisal is sometimes described as an exact science, artistically applied. There is always room for adjustment in determining the exact value of a property, and the temptation may arise to make the scientific data fit the wishes or needs of the customer.

Appraisers are no longer directly hired by the lender. In an effort to combat the accelerated values that are blamed for contributing to the financial crisis of the late 2000s, new legislation now requires the lender to make a request to an appraisal management company or to an in-house group of approved Fannie Mae/Freddie Mac appraisers that assigns on a rolling basis. No communication is allowed between the appraiser and the underwriter.

Lenders may still ask an appraiser to do a value check on a specific property. The lender can use this value check to determine loan-to-value, type of loan product to originate, and costs of loan and to quantify equity in a property. The NAR Code of

Ethics provides specific direction for this type of opinion of value. Appraisers performing a value check are technically performing an appraisal and should adhere to appraisal guidelines. However, it is unlikely that this appraisal will be allowed to be assigned for any Fannie Mae/Freddie Mac or HUD loan.

case study	## Case Study #8—Is It Worth It?

Paul, who is both a licensed appraiser and a REALTOR®, has listed his own home for sale. He has accepted an offer to purchase and needs to have an appraisal done to substantiate the price offered on the contract. Wanting to avoid any perception of conflict of interest, he has asked Helen, an appraiser friend and colleague, to do the appraisal. After viewing the property, Helen finds that the only way to reach the value stated in the contract would be to count some of the below-ground finished area of the house as ground-level living area. The space is in fact a finished recreation room that is regularly used as living space by the family, but Helen was uncomfortable giving it a higher financial value than was actually warranted. Despite her friend Paul's wish to just "squeeze it" a little, Helen decided that rather than misrepresent the subject of the appraisal—the house—she would refuse to do the appraisal.

For Discussion

1. Should an appraiser be allowed to do an appraisal on his own listing?

2. Is it appropriate for someone to be both an appraiser and a REALTOR®?

3. Is there any room to "squeeze" more value in an appraisal?

4. Should a REALTOR® ask a friend/colleague to do the appraisal on his own home?

Home Inspectors

The American Society of Home Inspectors (ASHI) has its own code of ethics. Although membership in ASHI is by choice, more and more states are requiring home inspectors to be licensed and to meet specific state regulations and standards. The overzealous inspector who figuratively tears the house apart, pointing out every minor dent and scratch as being near fatal, does no better job of serving the purchaser than does the lackadaisical one that overlooks major defects and potential problem areas. Home inspectors have been accused of deliberately killing the deal or suggesting to the purchasers that they should renegotiate the purchase price based on the inspection findings. Even with an inspection that is handled fairly and objectively, the buyers or sellers (or their agents) might distort the findings for their own benefit.

case study	## Case Study #9—Take It or Leave It?

Jim and Gail have a contract on the Wilsons' house that includes a home inspection contingency with a five-day negotiating period to follow the inspection. If no agreement is reached within the five-day period, either party may terminate the contract. On the first day after the inspection, the purchasers submit a list of repairs to be made at the sellers' expense. The sellers refuse to sign off on the repairs, and on the third day, the purchasers agree to drop the request and proceed to settlement without the repairs being done. On the fourth day, the sellers declare the contract terminated on the basis that they did not accept the first contract amendment, thereby voiding the contract.

For Discussion

1. Would it have made a difference if the purchasers had waited to submit the list of repairs until the last day of the contingency period?

2. Did the sellers have the right to refuse making the repairs?

3. Would the type of repairs requested have made a difference?

4. Was the list of repairs in fact an amendment that left the door open for the sellers to void the contract?

(In a similar actual case, legal counsel advised that the five-day period was clearly a negotiation period and that the purchasers had every right to proceed with the original contract.)

Settlement Agents

Depending on where in the country a property is located, the settlement or closing may be conducted by a real estate attorney, title and escrow company agent (East Coast and middle of the country), or in escrow in the western part of the United States. Generally, the closing occurs with nothing more than minor squabbles between the seller and the buyer over missing items, unfinished repairs, or faulty equipment. More serious problems may involve the financing, such as payment of discount points, misstated interest rate, or additional lender fees. In any case, the problems are generally between the parties involved—not with the settlement agent. The settlement agent's responsibility is to see that all terms of the contract are met, not to represent either of the parties to the transaction. If either buyers or sellers want to have representation, they must hire their own attorney.

One area of ethical concern with settlement agents is title insurance. Most lenders require that purchasers obtain title insurance protecting the lender's interest. Generally, the new homeowner is advised to also obtain owner's title insurance protecting the owner from any prior claims of interest on the property. If the settlement agent has any financial interest in the title insurance company, this must be disclosed.

All attorneys are subject to a code of ethics established long before REALTORS® even came into the picture, but occasionally there are still cases where the attorney has absconded with funds, made grievous errors, or committed fraud. In a recent case in central Florida, the title and escrow agent did not show up at the settlement table on time. He had just been handcuffed and led away to jail on charges of diverting monies received for settlement into his own account. A very scary period of sleepless nights followed for both seller and buyer as the settlement remained in limbo for weeks.

Some years ago in Virginia, legislation was proposed that would have mandated that only attorneys would be allowed to conduct real estate settlements. As the General Assembly deliberated, advocates for both attorneys and title and escrow companies presented their cases. The outcome of the hearings indicated that, while there was about an equal number of cases of unethical behavior, mismanagement, and blatant fraud on both sides, the majority of settlements took place in an ethical and professional manner regardless of who presided at the table. Just as over one million REALTORS® do not always act in an ethical manner, neither do all certified settlement agents. Unfortunately, there are sometimes rotten apples in the barrel.

Lenders

Contributor:

Doug Enger,
PrimeLending, A
PlainsCapital Co.,
Ashburn, VA

The Mortgage Bankers Association and the American Association of Mortgage Brokers both have a code of ethics to which all their lender members subscribe. The mortgage loan business is highly competitive, especially in large metro areas. The drive to originate more loans every day that will be profitable for the company (and the loan officer) can sometimes lead to unethical behavior.

Thanks to computerized automated lending, a loan officer can obtain approval on many loans in a matter of minutes. Much loan origination is actually done over the telephone with no face-to-face meeting with the borrower. The use of online lending grows daily. Major banks and myriad mortgage broker companies can take an application, process it, and finalize a loan all by computer. In many cases, this is beneficial, but sometimes there are potential problems. RESPA regulations are very strict about the borrower receiving a good-faith estimate with all estimated costs of settlement within three business days of application. The truth-in-lending statement, which must also be provided to the borrower, shows the actual cost of the credit being extended, including the annual percentage rate (APR). The APR is calculated by adding any discount points and lender fees to the amount received by the lender based on the agreed-upon interest rate for the loan. For example, a 6% interest rate may have an APR of 6.5% when the additional monies received by the lender are included. An unsuspecting borrower may be attracted by the low rate of interest but neglect to look at the APR. A 4% loan with an APR of 8% is a probable indication of extraneous fees or points being charged. A useful rule of thumb is that the APR should not be more than one-half to one point above the stated rate.

"A" paper describes the mortgage loan that a qualified borrower will receive. Borrowers who present a higher risk to the lender may be classified as "B" paper or even "C" or "D" in worst cases. The higher-risk loans require a higher rate of interest and possibly a larger down payment. If the borrower does, in fact, have credit problems and this is the only loan possible, this is perfectly justified. An ethical problem arises when a loan officer pushes an unknowing borrower into the higher-priced loan when it is not necessary. This is when lending becomes predatory.

Other examples of unethical behavior on the part of loan officers include

- looking the other way when a "gift" is, in fact, a secondary loan;
- allowing the borrower to overstate income;
- neglecting to include all debt liabilities;
- approving a loan for residential use when it is actually for investment;
- offering a lower rate of interest than is actually available;
- encouraging a potential borrower to "drop" its present loan officer;
- padding an appraisal to meet the contract price;
- adding unnecessary additional points or fees; and
- allowing the borrowers to "get in over their heads."

The last example is probably the most subtle one on the list. Every loan product has set guidelines for qualifying standards. But should all borrowers commit themselves to the limit of their capability?

Case Study #10—Up to the Limit

Joan and Billy both graduated with master's degrees from American University last spring and plan to be married in September. Joan has started her new job as a computer programmer at a biotech company specializing in stem cell research. Billy has begun his new employment as an assistant manager of a large Wal-Mart store. Their combined income of over $100,000 qualifies them to borrow approximately $343,000. Because they will have very little cash left after their wedding, their loan officer, James, has suggested a 100% financing, no-money-down loan. This will give them just what they need in order to buy the new town house they have fallen in love with. The house payment will be slightly over $2,000 per month. At this point, they meet the qualifying standards and James could legally approve them for the loan. Are there ethical considerations?

Things for James to consider include the following:

- The couple is presently living in a shared furnished apartment space for $600 a month.

- Presently living in the center city, they do not own a car. They will be moving ten miles outside the city with no public transportation available.

- Stem cell research is a controversial topic today—how secure is Joan's job?

- Both Joan and Billy will soon have to start paying back student loans.

- Joan confided to James that she has just turned 34 and is anxious to start a family.

Today, the prevalence of short sales (i.e., the lender agrees to accept less than the actual amount due on the mortgage loan) creates a situation where unethical behavior may occur on the part of the REALTOR®, as well as the lender. For example, a REALTOR® takes a listing where the lender has agreed to accept a short sale and then reveals the minimum amount that will be accepted to a potential buyer who happens to be a relative of the seller. The REALTOR® always has a responsibility to market a property to obtain the maximum benefit to the seller. In the case of a short sale, the lender is also a party to the sale and deserves the best efforts of the REALTOR®; anything less than this may be a violation of the Code of Ethics.

Global Real Estate Practitioners

It is a small world and getting smaller by the day thanks to tremendous advances in technology. More and more U.S. companies are expanding into European and Asian markets. Another growing phenomenon is that of foreign companies purchasing U.S. companies.

Hungry while sightseeing? U.S. franchises appear in cities all over the world. Take your pick—McDonald's, Pizza Hut, Dunkin' Donuts, and KFC. They're all there. Two large real estate franchises, RE/MAX and ERA, also have a presence overseas. So where does ethics fit into this growing global market? Customary, local business practice and local law can vary greatly from one country to another. For example, in Norway, the Supreme Court ruled that antidiscrimination laws do *not* cover real estate agents who sell private property. The decision was made as a result of a case where the broker advertised "only for whites" and "foreigners unwanted." So much for Article 10 of the NAR Code!

True/False Questions (Circle the correct answer)

1. T   F   All real estate settlements must be conducted by a licensed attorney.

2. T   F   Lender X has just placed Mr. Garcia in a "B" paper loan by convincing Garcia that he does not qualify for an "A" loan with a lower interest rate due to the fact that he is a recent immigrant to this country. Lender X is a predatory lender.

■ Conclusion

Ethics is recognized by state regulators and professional organizations in this country as an important issue in all aspects of real estate practice and for all real estate practitioners. Many ethical dilemmas revolve around agency and the responsibility of the agent to clients and customers. Ethical questions can arise with residential and commercial agents, property managers and leasing agents, appraisers, home inspectors, settlement agents, and lenders. One of the challenges for those engaged in global real estate practice is the problem of other cultures having a different interpretation of what constitutes ethical behavior.

■ Review Questions

1. *MOST* real estate practitioners come from a career background of
   a. sales.
   b. military.
   c. education.
   d. all of these.

2. ARELLO is the organization responsible for
   a. promoting uniform standards for administering and enforcing state license laws.
   b. requiring a good-faith estimate be given to all borrowers.
   c. making amendments to the NAR Code of Ethics.
   d. disclosing APR on real estate advertising.

3. For *MOST* people, the purchase of a home is
   a. accomplished at least four times in a lifetime.
   b. the largest investment they will ever make.
   c. beyond their financial capability.
   d. no longer considered important.

4. The required disclosure of agency relationship forced the issue of who an agent represented by declaring that the agent worked in the best interests of the
   a. buyer.
   b. seller.
   c. both buyer and seller.
   d. neither buyer nor seller.

5. The demand for true representation of the buyer began to grow in the
   a. late 1980s.
   b. early 1990s.
   c. mid-1990s.
   d. late 1990s.

6. One way to avoid a conflict of interest when two agents from the same firm are involved in the same transaction is for the agents to be
   a. dual agents.
   b. disclosed dual agents.
   c. designated agents.
   d. limited representatives.

7. Julio is representing both the seller and the buyer in the same transaction. In this case of disclosed dual agency, Julio has
   a. one customer.
   b. one client.
   c. two customers.
   d. two clients.

8. Having multiple clients is *MOST* likely to be a problem when they are all
   a. demanding of the agent's attention.
   b. interested in buying the same property.
   c. interested in four different geographic areas.
   d. qualified for the same price range.

9. In a commercial transaction, all of the following could create problems for the agent *EXCEPT*
   a. multiple players in one transaction.
   b. several transactions involved in one project.
   c. request of the buyer to remain anonymous.
   d. membership in more than one professional organization.

10. When multiple applications are received at the same time for a rental property, the decision to accept should be based on the applicant's
    a. religion.
    b. nationality.
    c. marital status.
    d. financial position.

11. Jack is a licensed appraiser as well as a REALTOR®. He will be expected to follow
    a. the NAR Code of Ethics.
    b. the Uniform Standards of Professional Appraisal Practice (USPAP).
    c. either the NAR Code of Ethics or USPAP.
    d. both the NAR Code of Ethics and USPAP.

12. All of the following statements regarding home inspectors are true *EXCEPT*
    a. home inspectors may choose to belong to ASHI.
    b. many states today require home inspectors to be licensed.
    c. an overzealous inspector causes as much problem as a lackadaisical one.
    d. home inspectors should encourage buyers to renegotiate the sales price.

13. All real estate settlements or closings must be conducted by

    a. an escrow agent.

    b. a real estate attorney.

    c. a title and escrow company.

    d. any of the above, depending on state law and local custom.

14. A lender can request a value check from an appraiser that can be used for all of the following *EXCEPT*

    a. determining loan-to-value.

    b. choosing the appropriate loan product.

    c. quantifying equity in a property.

    d. using as basis for Fannie Mae loan.

15. One of the biggest challenges for the expanding of the global real estate market is the difference in

    a. language.

    b. social customs.

    c. monetary system.

    d. interpretation of ethical behavior.

Review
Good Job!

chapter three

National Association of REALTORS® Code of Ethics

Learning Objectives

Upon completion of this chapter, you will be able to

- describe the origins of the National Association of REALTORS® Code of Ethics, the ethics training now required of all NAR members, and a brief summary of the NAR Pathways to Professionalism;

- provide examples of Articles 1-9 of the NAR Code – Duties to Clients & Customers;

- provide examples of Articles 10-12 of the NAR Code – Duties to the Public; and

- provide examples of Articles 13-17 of the NAR Code – Duties to REALTORS®.

■ Key Terms

agent	customer	Professional Standards Committee
arbitration	kickback	
client	living document	Standards of Practice (SOP)
competitive market analysis (CMA)	mediation	stigmatized property
	procuring cause	

■ Introduction

All new members of the National Association of REALTORS® (NAR) are required to take an orientation course that includes at least two-and-one-half hours of ethics. Unfortunately, this is not enough time to cover all of the 17 articles, plus the numerous Standards of Practice (SOP) that accompany the articles. A brief description of all the articles and some of the more significant SOPs is given in this chapter. An example of the NAR-recommended use of mediation in lieu of arbitration is also presented.

1. Learning Objective: Describe the origins of the National Association of REALTORS® Code of Ethics, the ethics training now required of all NAR members, and a brief summary of the NAR Pathways to Professionalism.

■ From the Beginning

When NAR was formed in the early 1900s, a primary goal of the association was to improve the business practices in place and to provide guidelines for ethical standards for the future. The REALTORS® were the first business group outside the professions of medicine, engineering, and law to adopt a code of ethics. The first code of ethics was written in 1913 and became a mandatory requirement for membership in 1924.

Historical Footnotes

In 2013, NAR celebrated the centennial of the Code of Ethics. Frederick Heller, manager of the virtual library and archives for NAR, pointed out some of the following highlights of the 100 years existence of the Code in the November issue of REALTOR®Mag, a NAR publication.

■ NAR was founded in 1908 as the National Association of Real Estate Exchanges (name changed to National Association of REALTORS® in 1972) and a special committee was created to develop a Code of Ethics. After five years of exploring how the concept of ethics could apply to the practice of real estate, the first two basic concepts were created: the broker's duty to clients and the duty to fellow brokers. The concept of duty to the general public was added later.

■ The NAR Code was not actually the first one that was prepared for real estate practitioners. The Greater Baltimore Board of REALTORS® incorporated rules of conduct into its bylaws when it was founded in 1858—the bylaws were specifically created to discourage members from stealing listings from each other! By 1913, many local associations had their own ethics code. The Kansas City Code was actually used as a model for the NAR version. Some local associations continued to develop their own codes until 1923, when the NAR bylaws were amended to require all local associations to adopt the national code.

■ In 1913, the conventional wording in documents was to use all male pronouns. It was not until 1989, when over half of the nation's REALTORS® were women, that gender-neutral phrasing became the norm.

In NAR's Info Central Blog of July 17, 2013, Heller also provided us with an interesting footnote to the birthday of the NAR Code. It was adopted on July 29, 1913, at the annual convention held in Winnipeg, Canada. At that time, many local and provincial real estate associations in Canada were members of NAR. The site of the annual convention was always a contest and in 1913 there were three candidates. The final selection became overtaken by a catastrophic event when three Winnipeg REALTORS® went down with the *R.M.S. Titanic* in April of 1912. The delegates to the 1912 convention chose Winnipeg for the 6th annual convention in their honor.

A Living Document

The code is described as a *living document* because it is carefully reviewed, amended, and/or edited every year by the NAR Professional Standards Committee. The articles and the Standards of Practice (SOP) that are included with many of the articles reflect the numerous changes in business practice and market conditions over the years. An SOP may be created to clarify the intent of an article, to reflect a change in market practices, or to provide an illustration or example of how the particular article is to be interpreted. Significant market changes such as the acceptance in residential brokerage of buyer agency can be seen in multiple adjustments made to the code in the mid-1990s. (Interesting to note there was an amendment made in 1928 to prohibit "horseback appraisals"!)

In the early years of the 21st century, NAR began to strongly encourage *mediation* in lieu of *arbitration* for contractual dispute resolution. While not actually a part of the Code of Ethics, mediation is discussed in more detail later in this chapter.

Required Ethics Training

Every article of the code is based on the original vision of its creators to better serve the public, using the code as the means to achieve that goal. As noted earlier, new members joining the tri-level local/state/national membership of NAR must take a two-and-one-half hour orientation course on the Code of Ethics and pledge to conduct their real estate practices professionally and ethically, as set forth in the code. The orientation course also satisfies the quadrennial training requirement for the first four-year cycle.

Effective January 1, 2001, all members of NAR are also required to complete a minimum of two-and-one-half hours of continuing education ethics training in every four-year cycle. Every real estate board and association must provide access to courses on ethics through classroom, correspondence, or internet-based instruction. This quadrennial training is also available online at the NAR website, www.realtor.org. The course includes all recent policy changes or additions, case studies, and a final exam requiring a score of 75% to receive credit.

Enforcement of the Code of Ethics is usually handled at the local level through hearing panels made up of members of the Professional Standards Committee. In some cases, a small board or association may opt to have the complaint handled by the state to avoid any question of conflict of interest. Guidelines for ethics and arbitration hearings are provided in the *NAR Code of Ethics and Arbitration Manual* published annually by NAR.

(See Appendix A for a copy of the Code of Ethics; easy reference to the actual printed code will be helpful in reviewing the articles of the code presented in this chapter.)

■ Pathways to Professionalism

In addition to the Code of Ethics, NAR also publishes *Pathways to Professionalism*. This list of professional courtesies is strictly voluntary and cannot be used as the basis for an alleged ethics violation complaint. It is offered in the hope of raising the standard of ethical and professional behavior in real estate practice. Local boards and associations can make additions, adjustments, or annotations relative to practice in their specific area.

The complete *Pathways to Professionalism* is reprinted here. You will note that the wording is much more definitive regarding specific actions to be taken, or avoided, by the real estate professional. As you read through them, ask yourself how many of these are now part of your regular practice of real estate; then look for others that you could start to include.

Respect for the Public

1. Follow the "Golden Rule": Do unto others as you would have them do unto you.
2. Respond promptly to inquiries and requests for information.
3. Schedule appointments and showings as far in advance as possible.
4. Call if you are delayed or must cancel an appointment or showing.
5. If a prospective buyer decides not to view an occupied home, promptly explain the situation to the listing broker or the occupant.
6. Communicate with all parties in a timely fashion.
7. When entering a property, ensure that unexpected situations, such as pets, are handled appropriately.
8. Leave your business card if not prohibited by local rules.
9. Never criticize property in the presence of the occupant.
10. Inform occupants that you are leaving after showings.
11. When showing an occupied home, always ring the doorbell or knock—and announce yourself loudly—before entering. Knock and announce yourself loudly before entering any closed room.
12. Present a professional appearance at all times; dress appropriately and drive a clean car.
13. If occupants are home during showings, ask their permission before using the telephone or bathroom.
14. Encourage the clients of other brokers to direct questions to their agent or representative.
15. Communicate clearly; don't use jargon or slang that may not be readily understood.
16. Be aware of and respect cultural differences.
17. Show courtesy and respect to everyone.
18. Be aware of—and meet—all deadlines.
19. Promise only what you can deliver—and keep your promises.
20. Identify your REALTOR® and your professional status in contacts with the public.
21. Do not tell people what you think—tell them what you know.

Respect for Property

1. Be responsible for everyone you allow to enter listed property.
2. Never allow buyers to enter listed property unaccompanied.
3. When showing property, keep all members of the group together.
4. Never allow unaccompanied access to property without permission.
5. Enter property only with permission even if you have a lockbox key or combination.
6. When the occupant is absent, leave the property as you found it (lights, heating, cooling, drapes, etc.). If you think something is amiss (e.g. vandalism), contact the listing broker immediately.
7. Be considerate of the seller's property. Do not allow anyone to eat, drink, smoke, dispose of trash, use bathing or sleeping facilities, or bring pets. Leave the house as you found it unless instructed otherwise.
8. Use sidewalks; if weather is bad, take off shoes and boots inside property.
9. Respect sellers' instructions about photographing or videographing their properties' interiors or exteriors. (Added 11/13)

Respect for Peers

1. Identify your REALTOR® and professional status in all contacts with other REALTORS®.
2. Respond to other agents' calls, faxes, and emails promptly and courteously.
3. Be aware that large electronic files with attachments or lengthy faxes may be a burden on recipients.
4. Notify the listing broker if there appears to be inaccurate information on the listing.
5. Share important information about a property, including the presence of pets, security systems, and whether sellers will be present during the showing.
6. Show courtesy, trust, and respect to other real estate professionals.
7. Avoid the inappropriate use of endearments or other denigrating language.
8. Do not prospect at other REALTORS®' open houses or similar events.
9. Return keys promptly.
10. Carefully replace keys in the lockbox after showings.
11. To be successful in the business, mutual respect is essential.
12. Real estate is a reputation business. What you do today may affect your reputation—and business—for years to come.

(Source: Reproduced with permission of the National Association of REALTORS®. Copyright 2008. Revised 2013. All rights reserved.)

The Association of West/South Suburban Chicagoland has brought the NAR *Pathways to Professionalism* to life in a 15-minute video presentation available on YouTube under Mainstreet Organization of REALTORS® (MORe), January, 2012.

True/False Questions (Circle the correct answer)

1. T   F   In the first year of membership in NAR, the REALTOR® must take a 2½ hour orientation course plus an additional 2½ hours to meet the quadrennial requirement.

2. T   F   Being aware that sending large electronic files with attachments may be a burden to recipients is included in the Pathways to Professionalism as showing respect for the public.

2. Learning Objective: Provide examples of Articles 1-9 of the NAR Code – Duties to Clients & Customers.

■ The NAR Code of Ethics

The original Code of Ethics contained 22 articles. In the early 1970s, a decision was made to move five of the articles to the preamble. The remaining 17 articles were then grouped into three categories: Duties to Clients and Customers, Duties to the Public, and Duties to REALTORS®.

The Preamble

The preamble contains the aspirational aspects of the code. The ideals set forth in the preamble are not mandatory nor subject to sanction as are the 17 articles of the code; rather, they serve as a model for professional behavior. REALTORS® are challenged to

- maintain and improve the standards of their calling;
- share with their fellow REALTORS® a common responsibility for integrity and honor;
- strive to become and remain informed on issues affecting real estate;
- share their experience and study with others;
- assist regulatory bodies in eliminating practices that may damage the public or discredit or dishonor the real estate profession;
- bring to the attention of the appropriate Board or Association of REAL-TORS® conduct involving misappropriation of client or customer funds or property, willful discrimination, or fraud resulting in substantial economic harm;
- urge exclusive representation of clients;
- avoid attempting to gain unfair advantage over competitors;
- refrain from making unsolicited comments about other practitioners;
- offer objective opinions not influenced by personal motivation or gain; and
- follow the Golden Rule.

The opening words of the preamble to the Code of Ethics are as relevant today as when they were first written.

"Under all is the land. Upon its wise utilization and widely allocated owner-ship depend the survival and growth of free institutions and of our civilization. REALTORS® should recognize that the interests of the union and its citizens require the highest and best use of the land and the widest distribution of land ownership. They require the creation of adequate housing, the building of functioning cities, the development of productive industries and farms, and the preservation of a healthful environment."

Suggestions for changes to the wording have been made over the years, but the decision has always been to retain them just as they were first written.

Duties to Clients and Customers

The first nine articles identify the REALTOR®'s responsibility to clients and customers. Articles 1, 2, and 9 are especially important and are among those frequently cited for violation.

Article 1—Protecting the Client

Article 1 concentrates on the responsibility to protect and promote the interests of the client, while still treating all parties honestly. There are 16 **Standards of Practice** attached to Article 1, many of which reflect changes made necessary as a result of the growing importance of buyer agency. Some of the most relevant SOPs are listed here along with case examples.

SOP 1-2 states the duties imposed by the Code of Ethics encompass all real estate–related activities and transactions, whether conducted in person, electronically, or through any other means. This SOP also provides clear definitions for the following:

- **Client**—the person with whom the REALTOR® has an agency relationship or legally recognized non-agent relationship

  Example: Buyer B has a signed buyer agency agreement with REALTOR® A. Buyer B is a client. Seller D has a signed listing agreement with REALTOR® C. Seller D is a client.

- **Customer**—a party to the transaction who receives information, services, or benefits but has no contractual relationship with the REALTOR®

  Example: Mr. and Mrs. Potential Buyers visit an open house held by REALTOR® A. They are customers unless they actually discuss the purchase of that property and engage REALTOR® A to represent them.

- **Agent**—licensee (including brokers and sales associates) acting in an agency relationship as defined by state law or regulation

  Example: REALTOR® A is affiliated with ABC brokerage firm and can work as either a listing agent or buyer agent. (State laws vary as to exact agency status.) The broker of the firm is also referred to as the agent of the clients.

- **Broker**—licensee (including brokers and sales associates) acting as an agent or in a legally recognized non-agency capacity

  Example: REALTOR® B has completed additional real estate education and can be proprietor of own sales firm or be affiliated with another firm.

Other Standards of Practice prohibit misleading an owner regarding market value (SOP 1-3) or misleading buyers as to perceived benefits gained by using the service of that particular REALTOR® (SOP 1-4). The question of how long the REALTOR® must continue to present offers or counteroffers is covered in SOPs 1-7 and 1-8. The issue of confidentiality and how long information must remain confidential is fully covered in SOP 1-9, which also states that disclosure of latent material defects is not considered disclosure of confidential information.

Example: Most states require disclosure of material defects in the property. REALTOR® A is correct in disclosing the history of a wet basement to potential buyers even if the seller wishes to keep it a secret since it is now August and the basement is dry.

Specific information that must be provided prior to entering into either listing or buyer agency agreements is itemized in SOPs 1-12 and 1-13. SOP1-15 specifies the conditions under which existing offers on a property may be disclosed. The most recent SOP, 1-16, specifically states that REALTORS® cannot access or use listed or managed property under any conditions not authorized by the owner.

Example: The sellers of REALTOR® B's listing have already moved to the West Coast. Settlement is scheduled for February 2 using a power-of-attorney for the sellers. The buyers have to move out of their rental apartment on January 31 and have requested to move their furniture to the garage on that day. Since the house and garage are empty, REALTOR B assumes this would be okay. In fact, it should not be allowed without the written consent of the owners and would be a potential violation of Article 1.

Article 2—Disclosure

Article 2 has very few SOPs but often becomes a critical issue in real-life practice because it deals with misrepresentation or concealment of pertinent facts relating to the property or the transaction. Commonly heard complaints are as follows:

- "You didn't tell me the street was to be widened right in front of my door!"
- "There was no hardwood floor under where the dining room carpet used to be!"
- "They're bulldozing the trees behind my house!"
- "The neighbors tell me there is a ghost in the attic!"

In almost every state, disclosure of adverse material facts related to the physical condition of the property must be disclosed. Disclosure of facts related to the transaction becomes a gray issue, depending on the interpretation of the word *transaction*. SOP 2-5 says that factors defined as *nonmaterial* by law or regulation are not considered pertinent for the purposes of Article 2. Ghosts and other stigmatized property issues may depend on the state in which the property is located. Some states require disclosure of stigmatizing facts like suicide, murder, or other felonies committed on the property. In other states, only material facts relating to the physical condition of the property require disclosure. The Code of Ethics is never to be used in opposition to the law but rather to support the law by bringing a higher sensitivity to its duties and responsibilities.

Example: REALTOR® A just listed an old Victorian home out on the edge of town that has been called "the haunted house" for years. The owner, a 94-year-old widow, is moving to an assisted-living home. Will REALTOR® A have to disclose the "ghosts"? It depends on where the house is located: in California, the presence of ghosts must be disclosed. In Virginia, the state law considers this to be a "non-material" fact requiring no disclosure. In Massachusetts, the fact that a property is considered to be "psychologically impacted" is not considered a material fact requiring disclosure; however, a REALTOR® from Salem, Massachusetts, once said that having a reported ghost in a historic property is actually considered a plus in their marketplace!

Article 3—Cooperation

Article 3 focuses on cooperation with other brokers. The article itself was amended in 1995. Most of the SOP was attached to the article in the mid-1990s, as buyer agency gained acceptance. It became important to make it clear that an offer of cooperation (via MLS) does not automatically make an offer of compensation. SOP 3-2 expands this to say that any change of compensation for cooperative services from other REALTORS® should be communicated *prior* to the time an offer to purchase is made. This was amended in 2014 to state that the listing broker cannot change the terms after an offer to purchase or lease has been made. A more recent SOP, 3-4, obligates a listing broker to disclose the existence of dual or variable rate commission arrangements when the commission offered to a buyer agent is different from that to be paid if the listing broker procures the sale. SOP 3-9, similar to SOP 1-16, reiterates that REALTORS® shall not provide access to listed property on terms other than those established by the owner or the listing broker.

Example: Broker A has a listing on Park Place that was just sold by one of his agents. Another contract has been received and is to be presented at the same time to the sellers. Broker A tells the sellers that if they accept the offer presented by his own agent, he will reduce the commission; if they accept the other company's offer, the commission will remain the same as stated in the MLS. This would be a variable rate of commission which should have been disclosed in the original listing.

Articles 4 and 5—Personal Interest

Both of these articles require REALTORS® to disclose their personal interest in the outcome of the transaction, whether buying or selling on their own account, for members of their immediate family, their firms, or any entities in which they have an ownership interest. Article 5 expands the disclosure requirement to include disclosure of any present or contemplated interest before providing professional services.

Example: REALTOR® D has listed a five-building apartment project. The fact that when the property is sold REALTOR® D will be named as the property manager needs to be disclosed (contemplated interest).

Article 6—No Kickbacks

Article 6 states that no commission, rebate, or profit may be accepted by the REALTOR® without the client's knowledge and consent. This article often leads to a discussion of Real Estate Settlement Procedures Act (RESPA) regulations that mandate that no agent may receive payment unless an actual service is rendered. This federal prohibition against kickbacks becomes critical when a REALTOR® is offered payment for referring clients to a particular lender, settlement agent, inspector, or home warranty program. Both Article 6 and RESPA regulations can become an issue when a brokerage firm offers one-stop shopping, concierge assistance, property management, and other related real estate services.

The House of Representatives passed legislation in 2012 that would have made the sale of a home warranty exempt from the RESPA regulations, but it was never passed by the Senate. HUD's interpretation remains that no fee can be paid unless an actual service is rendered, not merely a referral.

Example: A loan officer has offered to provide the refreshments for REALTOR® C's open house. This is only permissible if this is to be a joint marketing effort for both the lender and the REALTOR®—sharing in all expenses including refreshments and advertising with both lender and REALTOR® present at the open house to meet and greet.

Articles 7 and 8—Commissions and Escrow

These two articles are both concerned with money. In Article 7, the REALTOR® is prohibited from accepting commission from more than one party to the transaction without disclosure and informed consent of all parties. This became significant when the buyer agent was to be paid through the transaction from funds paid by a seller to the listing broker. Article 8 is directed primarily to principal brokers, requiring that all monies retained by the broker in trust for other persons must be held in a special account separate from their own funds. State regulator rules and regulations have specific criteria for how these funds are recorded, applied, or released from trust or escrow.

Example: Broker REALTOR® G is holding in an escrow account a $20,000 earnest money deposit on a property that recently sold for $200,000. At settlement, REALTOR® G will receive $6,000 in commission. Coming up a little short on available cash to pay this month's bills, REALTOR® G "borrows" $3,000 from the escrow account rationalizing that this amount would be paid to the broker's account within the next 30 days. This is a direct violation of the Code of Ethics and also of state law in most states.

Article 9—Get It in Writing!

A relatively simple statement with only two SOPs, this article is one that is often found to be in violation. To "get it in writing" should be fairly obvious, but many cases of violations of both ethics and state regulations revolve around the question of who said what to whom and when. Failure to obtain everything in writing can occur during the original ratification process or when subsequent changes, additions, or corrections are made. Another frequent source of complaint is the failure to obtain extensions when dates specified in the original contract are not going to be met. In all cases, a copy of the signed or initialed agreement must be given to all parties immediately upon signing. SOP 9-2 was added in 2007 and stresses the need for REALTORS® to explain the nature and disclose the specific terms of all contractual relationships being established electronically prior to acceptance by the contracting party. Many printed contracts today include a paragraph granting permission for all documents and required notices to be made electronically, including signatures.

Example: The offer to purchase was accepted and ratified by all parties on March 1, with a projected settlement date of May 1. On April 1, the sellers asked to extend the settlement date to June 1 because their new home was not going to be finished until that date. The buyers orally agreed but no addendum was ever prepared and signed by all parties. When the buyers found that they were not able to extend their rental agreement for the extra month they insisted on settling on the original date of May 1. The sellers must follow through on the original date specified in the contract or could be subject to court action.

True/False Questions (Circle the correct answer)

1.   T   F   REALTOR® C has a new listing where the previous owners were murdered during an attempted burglary of their home. Regardless of where the property is located, REALTOR® C will be required to disclose this information.

2.   T   F   The listing broker has the right to change the offer of compensation to a cooperating broker at any time prior to the settlement date.

3. Learning Objective: Provide examples of Articles 10-14 of the NAR Code – Duties to the Public.

Duties to the Public

Articles 10 through 14 constitute this section and are concerned with general dealings with the public as opposed to the direct dealings with clients and customers as outlined in the first group of articles.

Article 10—Discrimination

This "equal opportunity in housing" article reiterates the federal, state, and local laws that prohibit denial of professional service to anyone on the basis of race, color, religion, national origin, sex, handicap, or familial status. Real estate professionals must provide equal professional service for every person seeking to either rent or purchase housing. (The federal fair housing laws do not apply to commercial or nonresidential real estate transactions, but some states do include commercial transactions in their state fair housing laws.) Article 10 has also been extended to include equal opportunity employment of both agents and administrative staff. In 2005, SOP 10-1, 10-2, and 10-3 were amended or adopted to discuss how the volunteering of demographic information and advertising statements should be handled to avoid any possibility of discrimination. SOP 10-2 specifically allows REALTORS® not involved in a residential transaction to provide demographic information under certain circumstances.

In January 2011, NAR went beyond federal fair housing law and included sexual orientation in the list of classes to be protected from the denial of professional services and in employment practices. In 2014, Article 10 was further amended to include gender identity in the list of protected classes. SOP 10-3 was also amended to reflect that no discrimination would be made in printed, displayed, or circulated statements or advertisements against persons based on sexual orientation.

Article 11—Area of Expertise

REALTORS® are sometimes asked to handle transactions that are basically out of their fields of expertise. Article 11 admonishes the REALTORS® to stick to the areas that are within their fields of competence. The higher commission on a large commercial transaction is always appealing, but a residential agent with no real knowledge of commercial transactions would far better serve the clients by referring them to a commercial agent. One other option offered in Article 11 is to engage the assistance of someone competent in the particular field of interest, thereby retaining the relationship with the client while offering the care and protection required.

An important part of every REALTOR®'s job is to prepare a competitive market analysis (CMA) to assist a seller client in setting a list price or to provide current market information to a potential buyer. Occasionally, the REALTOR® may be asked to provide an opinion of value or price on a property that is not part of the usual listing or selling process. In this case, SOP 11-1 specifies exactly what should be included in this opinion of value. This SOP was further revised in 2014 to include the provision that REALTORS® must

1. be knowledgeable about the type of property being valued,
2. have access to the information and resources necessary to formulate an accurate opinion, and
3. be familiar with the area where the subject property is located unless lack of any of these is disclosed to the party requesting the opinion in advance.

The following additional disclosure requirements were also added in 2014:

- Disclosure of whether and when a physical inspection of the property's exterior was conducted

- Disclosure of whether and when a physical inspection of the property's interior was conducted

- Disclosure of whether the REALTOR® has any conflicts of interest

It is important that such opinion of value not be construed as an appraisal. Appraisals must be prepared by a licensed or certified appraiser

Article 12—Advertising

Article 12 tells REALTORS® to be honest and truthful in their real estate communications and to always present a true picture in their advertising and representations to the public. This article did not require much further explanation until buyer agency came into the picture. Now SOP 12-1, 12-2, and 12-3 all relate to how an agent may advertise free service and/or premiums, prizes, or discounts as inducements to list or sell with that agent. The important issue is that full disclosure be made of what must be done to receive the benefit. SOP 12-5 requires that the name of the firm be given in all advertising of real estate services or listed properties in any medium (e.g., electronically, print, radio, television, and so on). It does exempt electronic displays of limited information such as texts, tweets, and thumbnails as long as they are linked to a display that does include all required disclosures. SOP 12-7 created quite a stir when amended in 1996 to allow the selling broker to also advertise, claiming to have sold the property. Some listing brokers still erroneously think they alone have the right to run that advertisement. SOPs 12-8, 12-9, 12-10, and 12-11 were added in 2007, covering the presentation of a true picture in advertising on REALTOR® internet content. SOP 12-10 was amended in 2013 to specifically prohibit presenting content developed by others without either attribution or permission or to otherwise mislead consumers. SOPs 12-12 and SOP 12-13 were added in 2008 and refer to use of URLs or domain names and the display of professional designations.

Example: REALTOR® B considers the Royal Palms subdivision to be his special area of expertise. He has had numerous listings and sales in the community over the past five years. Yesterday, he posted pictures and information on Facebook and on his personal website of six homes currently on sale in Royal Palms. Unfortunately, two of the properties shown were listed by a different broker and he has now had a complaint filed against him, citing Article 12.

Article 13—Don't Practice Law

This one is really easy—do not practice law. Recommend that legal counsel be obtained if questions arise during the transaction that are beyond the scope of the agent.

Example: REALTOR® D thought she was just being helpful when she advised her clients the best way to take title to the property they were purchasing. Providing information on the different ways to hold an interest in property is acceptable, but giving actual legal advice on how to act is not.

Article 14—Code Enforcement

This article and its accompanying SOP are all related to the REALTOR®'s obligation to cooperate with the appropriate board or association whenever charged with unethical practice. This obligation also includes the duty to give testimony or appear as a witness if called upon and to take no action to obstruct or disrupt the process.

Example: REALTOR® C was angry when he received notification that an ethics complaint had been filed with his local association. Considering the whole thing ridiculous, he refused to respond to the charge or to attend a panel hearing. He was found not only in violation of the Article that was referred to in the complaint but also with a violation of Article 14 for not cooperating with the investigation.

True/False Questions (Circle the correct answer)

1.   T   F   Broker D has opened a new office in a part of the city that is predominantly populated by immigrants from Central America. As long as he only hires agents from Costa Rica, Guatemala, Panama, Belize, El Salvador, Honduras, and Nicaragua, he will not be in violation of Article 10.

2.   T   F   Salesperson Francesco was the buyer agent on the sale of 1234 Elm Avenue. After settlement, he ran an ad in his local paper claiming to have sold that property. The listing agent for 1234 Elm Avenue would be justified in filing an ethics complaint against Francesco.

4. Learning Objective: Provide examples of Articles 15-17 of the NAR Code – Duties to REALTORS®.

Duties to REALTORS®

Articles 15 to 17 are concerned with how REALTORS® act toward their fellow REALTORS®.

Article 15—Competitors

Mothers often say, "If you can't say something good, don't say anything at all." This is the gist of Article 15: make no false or misleading statements about other real estate professionals, their business, or their business practices. REALTORS® should concentrate on their own abilities and experience, while presenting their personal plan to provide the best service to the client. SOPs 15-2 and 15-3 were adopted in 2010 and clarify that REALTORS® must not repeat or republish negative statements made by others, whether in person, in writing, or on the internet and must remove such statements if known to be false. In 2012, Article 15 and SOPs 15-2 and 15-3 were amended to say "other real estate professionals," instead of "competitors."

Example: REALTOR® T is in competition with REALTOR® Z for a listing on Oakview Drive. During her interview with the sellers, Mrs. Seller asks REALTOR® T if she knows REALTOR® Z. The seller mentions that they will interviewing him later in the week. REALTOR® T's response is "Well, I can't say I actually know him, but I have heard that he had to respond a few weeks ago to a complaint for an ethics violation—something about lack of disclosure, or something. But, I don't really know that for a fact." REALTOR® T may have thought she was only passing along something said by others, but she was in fact, violating Article 15.

Article 16—Representation

One of the shortest articles:

"REALTORS® shall not engage in any practice or take any action inconsistent with exclusive representation or exclusive brokerage relationship agreements that other REALTORS® have with clients."

This sounds so simple, but in fact there are a total of 20 SOPs attached to this article. It has obviously needed much further explanation, example, and discussion. A brief description of the 20 SOP topics follows. Many of the Article 16 SOPs are also directly related to other Articles in the Code. The Duties to Clients and Customers and the way that representation of Clients and Customers is carried out are inevitably connected. A review of the following topics will probably remind the reader of one or more occasions in real life where an agent has violated Article 16 by acting inappropriately. Ironically, this is not the article most often cited in violation; although it may well be the one that impacts most REALTORS® in their day-to-day practice. All too often, busy agents complain about a lack of ethical behavior among their colleagues but are not willing to take the time and effort to help enforce the code. The only way for those who wish to upgrade the level of ethical business practice in their market area is to take the initiative to report apparent violations of the code to the local board or association. Mandatory ethics training may help, but as stated earlier, reading about ethics does not guarantee ethical behavior. Ethical business practice only results from dedicated professionals working together to raise and maintain quality standards of ethical business behavior.

SOP Topics in Article 16

SOP 16-1—aggressive and innovative business practices

SOP 16-2—general telephone canvass or mailing distribution

SOP 16-3—contacting client to offer different service

SOP 16-4—soliciting another's listing

SOP 16-5—soliciting another's buyer client

SOP 16-6—contact from another's client

SOP 16-7—client's future business

SOP 16-8—subsequent agreement after expiration of prior agreement

SOP 16-9—determining if prospect has exclusive agreement

SOP 16-10—disclosure of brokerage relationship to seller/landlord

SOP 16-11—disclosure to FSBO, request for compensation

SOP 16-12—disclosure of brokerage relationship to buyer/tenant

SOP 16-13—all dealings with client's representative

SOP 16-14—obligating client for additional commission

SOP 16-15—compensation through principal broker

SOP 16-16—modifying offer of compensation

SOP 16-17—extending offer of cooperation and/or compensation

SOP 16-18—using information from MLS to create referrals

SOP 16-19—placement of sign on property

SOP 16-20—inducing clients to cancel contractual agreements

Example: The most recent SOP added to further clarify Article 16 concerns the actions of a REALTOR® who leaves one brokerage firm for another. Since REALTOR® Q was the one who went out and secured the listing on Cherry Drive, he feels that it belongs to him and he should have the right to encourage the sellers to cancel with his old firm, and relist with his new one. However, all listings are in fact an agreement with the brokerage firm and REALTOR® Q would be in direct violation of Article 16 to encourage these sellers to make such a move.

Article 17—Arbitration

Article 17 is similar to Article 14, which required REALTORS® to cooperate with their local board or association's investigation if charged with an ethical violation. Article 17 requires resolution of money disputes through arbitration rather than through litigation. A local board or association can mandate that its members attempt to mediate a dispute before submitting to arbitration.

SOP 17-2 was amended in 2012 to say that declining to participate in mediation does not relieve REALTORS® of the duty to arbitrate. It also states that REALTORS® are not obliged to mediate or arbitrate in cases where all parties choose to not mediate or arbitrate.

Violations of Article 3 (Cooperation) and Article 16 (Representation) occasionally lead to contractual disputes between different firms. These disputes must be submitted to the arbitration process rather than taken to court. Arbitration hearings always deal with money (usually commissions), are between REALTOR® brokerage firms, and yield binding results. The hearings are held according to NAR-stated procedures at the local or state board or association.

SOP 17-4 lists specific noncontractual disputes that are also subject to arbitration. Adopted in 1997, this SOP involves compensation issues between cooperating brokers and cases where the agent is paid directly by the client. The determining factor in arbitration cases is procuring cause. For purposes of arbitration conducted by boards and associations of REALTORS®, procuring cause is understood as the uninterrupted series of events that result in a successful transaction, that is, a sale that closes or a lease that is executed. This SOP was amended in 2007 to include arbitration between two or more cooperating brokers where the listing broker is not a party. SOP 17-5 was added in 2007 requiring the REALTOR® requesting arbitration to agree to submit to the jurisdiction of the respondent's REALTOR® association when the dispute is between REALTORS® in different states.

A typical case presented for arbitration might involve a listing agent who showed the property and prepared and subsequently presented a contract that was accepted and went to settlement. Then another agent with a signed buyer-agency agreement showed up claiming to be entitled to the commission. The hearing panel must take into consideration many factors, including the nature of the transaction and all agreements, the role and relationship of all parties, initial contacts and conduct, and continuity or breaks in continuity. Generally, the REALTOR® who is able to present the stronger case for being the procuring cause of the transaction will prevail.

Example: REALTOR® A and REALTOR® B are in dispute over who initiated and carried through the procedures that led to a successful transaction (one that goes to settlement) for the sale of 1000 Elm Drive. REALTOR® A is preparing to file a suit in civil court rather than submit to arbitration. Legally, he has the right to file suit, but ethically, as a REALTOR®, he has agreed to submit such disputes to arbitration rather than civil court action. REALTOR® A would be subject to a possible violation of Article 17.

Mediation

An alternative to arbitration (discussed under Article 17) that is being actively promoted by NAR is mediation. All boards and associations are required to offer mediation as a way to resolve disputes, promote amicable resolutions, and reduce the number of cases requiring attention by the members of the Professional Standards Committee. The goal of mediation is for the parties involved to work out their own solution with the assistance of a neutral facilitator. If mediation fails, the complainant (or requestor) can still file for an arbitration hearing. Mediation procedures are outlined in the *NAR Code of Ethics and Arbitration Manual*.

| case study | **Case Study #1—Solving Your Own Problem** |

Broker Joan has a listing at 1234 Orchard Street. Salesperson Mark from broker Sally's office showed the property to the Evergreens in May, but they did not write a contract. In June, the Evergreens came to an open house, noted that the price had been dropped $10,000, and asked Joan to prepare a purchase offer for them. Their offer was accepted and settlement occurred on July 10 with broker Joan being paid the full commission.

On July 11, broker Sally called the local association to file a request for arbitration. She felt her company was entitled to the selling portion of the commission because her agent Mark had been the first to show the Evergreens the property, plus he had a signed buyer-agency agreement with the Evergreens. The local professional standards representative suggested they try mediation first and arranged for broker Joan and broker Sally to meet with mediator Jordan. At the mediation, both Joan and Sally were given an opportunity to present their sides of the case. Broker Sally argued that her agent Mark had a signed buyer agency agreement with the Evergreens which showed that he was entitled to a commission when they purchased a home. She also argued that Mark was the first person to introduce the Evergreens to the property. Broker Joan argued that her action of preparing the actual purchase offer was what led to the completion of the transaction, not the fact that they had seen the property earlier with Mark.

The mediator's role is to facilitate an agreement between the parties, not to resolve the issue. In an arbitration hearing, the panel will decide which of the parties was the procuring cause that led to the sale and settlement and will award the disputed commission to that broker. In most cases, an arbitration hearing does not split a commission but awards the total amount to one broker. In mediation, the disputing parties have an opportunity to work out their own solution.

Mediator Jordan provided a calm, reasonable atmosphere for both parties to make their case. After about an hour of negotiation, the two brokers were able to reach a compromise position. Broker Joan agreed to pay 40% of the selling side of the commission to broker Sally, which she would then share with her agent Mark. If the two brokers had not been able to reach an agreement, broker Sally could still have filed for arbitration.

For Discussion

1. Do you think this was a fair solution?

2. What do you think the result would have been if the case had gone to arbitration?

3. Could Agent Mark have done anything differently to protect his commission?

4. Was Broker Sally's decision fair to Agent Mark?

Case Study Questions

1. In this case, all of the following actions might have been given consideration to help determine procuring cause *EXCEPT*
   a. having a signed buyer agency agreement.
   b. being first to introduce the buyers to the property.
   c. writing the offer to purchase.
   d. agreeing to mediation.

2. The role of the mediator is to
   a. determine procuring cause.
   b. determine the resolution of the dispute.
   c. provide an atmosphere of cooperation between the parties.
   d. preside like a judge in civil court.

True/False Questions (Circle the correct answer)

1. T **F** Jane is a friend of salesperson Sylvia. Jane tells Sylvia to call her friend Jack because Jack has said he is very displeased with his listing agent, and Jane knows that he would like to work with Sylvia. Sylvia would be in violation of the Code of Ethics if she makes the call to Jack.

2. T **F** Broker Tom believes that he has a strong case for being the procuring cause for the sale of 1000 Ocean Avenue and is not willing to negotiate any part of the commission. He should definitely agree to go for mediation. *ARBITRATE*

■ Conclusion

The National Association of REALTORS® developed a Code of Ethics in 1913 that became a mandatory requirement for membership in 1924. NAR members are now required to take a minimum of 2½ hours of ethics training in every four-year period. There is also a requirement for all new members of the association to complete 2½ hours of ethics training as part of their initial orientation.

In addition to the Code of Ethics, NAR also provides *Pathways to Professionalism,* a list of professional courtesies that may be adopted by a local board or association with appropriate additions or adjustments to suit that particular market area. The NAR code is reviewed annually in order to respond to changes in real estate business practice such as buyer agency. The code is divided into three sections: Duties to Clients and Customers, Duties to the Public, and Duties to REALTORS®. Each of the 17 articles contains additional guidance in the form of Standards of Practice that help to describe, further explain, or give examples of the ethical behavior required under a particular article.

NAR now requires all boards and associations to offer mediation as an alternative to arbitration. With arbitration, a hearing panel will determine who was the procuring cause of the transaction and award the disputed funds to that person. Through mediation, the parties involved in the dispute are encouraged to work out their own solution, which may involve some splitting of the amount based on the contribution of both parties to the successful transaction.

■ Review Questions

1. Pledging to follow the REALTOR® Code of Ethics has been mandatory for membership in the National Association of REALTORS® since
   a. 1908.
   b. 1913.
   c. 1924.
   d. 1980.

2. Jack has been a member of NAR for ten years. He is now required to take
   a. 2½ hours of ethics training every year.
   b. 2½ hours of ethics training every two years.
   c. 2½ hours of ethics training every four years.
   d. three hours of ethics training every four years

3. The first REALTOR® association to incorporate rules of conduct into their bylaws was the
   a. Winnipeg, Canada Real Estate Exchange.
   b. Greater Baltimore Board of REALTORS®.
   c. Kansas City Board of REALTORS®.
   d. National Association of REALTORS®.

4. When the NAR Code of Ethics is referred to as a "living document," that means the code
   a. only applies to currently living people.
   b. is carefully reviewed and edited where necessary annually.
   c. is rewritten every year.
   d. is now available on the internet.

5. Which of the following statements concerning the Pathways to Professionalism is *TRUE*?
   a. The Pathways to Professionalism are a part of the NAR Code of Ethics.
   b. Subscribing to the Pathways to Professionalism is required of all NAR members.
   c. The Pathways to Professionalism include a list of professional courtesies with respect to the public, property, and peers.
   d. Failing to observe the Pathways to Professionalism can be used as the basis for an ethics violation.

6. Salesperson George is a little confused about whether he has any responsibility to a person wishing to purchase the property that he has listed. He should look at which of the following articles?
   a. Article 1
   b. Article 2
   c. Article 9
   d. Article 16

7. Broker Carlos is holding a $10,000 earnest money deposit for Mr. and Mrs. Taylor. Because this money is part of a real estate transaction, he must retain the funds in
   a. his business operating account.
   b. the company's escrow account.
   c. the type of separate account specified by his state law.
   d. his personal account, for up to one month.

8. When a case ends up in civil court, the first thing the judge will usually ask is "what does the contract say?" The importance of having every detail of a sales transaction in writing and signed by all parties is covered in
   a. Article 1.
   b. Article 2.
   c. Article 6.
   d. Article 9.

9. Article 10 is sometimes referred to as the "fair housing article" because it prohibits REALTORS® from denying professional services to anyone based on any of the following *EXCEPT*
   a. religion.
   b. nationality.
   c. profession.
   d. gender identify.

10. As of 2014, a REALTOR® providing an opinion of value (not an appraisal) for a bank must include all of the following *EXCEPT*

    a. disclosure of whether and when a physical inspection of the property's exterior was conducted.

    b. disclosure of whether and when a physical inspection of the property's interior was conducted.

    c. disclosure of whether the REALTOR® has any conflicts of interest.

    d. disclosure of whether there are any stigmatizing factors apparent in the property.

11. The name of the firm is required on almost all advertising but could be left out on

    a. an email.

    b. a tweet.

    c. a TV commercial.

    d. a newspaper ad.

12. REALTOR® C is making a listing presentation in hopes of securing a new seller client. She should stress all of the following *EXCEPT*

    a. her own selling abilities.

    b. her years of experience.

    c. her personal plan for marketing the property.

    d. her personal knowledge about her competitors.

13. Article 16 deals with the day-to-day practice of real estate, specifically with the area of representation of clients. All of the following are SOPs attached to this article *EXCEPT*

    a. aggressive and innovative business practices.

    b. contacting another agent's client.

    c. disclosure of latent defects.

    d. compensation through principal broker.

14. In an arbitration hearing, the panel will determine which agent was the procuring cause of the successful transaction based on who

    a. first showed the property.

    b. actually wrote the contract.

    c. has a signed buyer-agency agreement.

    d. initiated an uninterrupted series of events leading to the sale.

15. Which of the following is *NOT* typical of an arbitration hearing?

    a. The dispute involves a commission.

    b. Two principal brokers are involved.

    c. An attempt at mediation will follow the arbitration hearing.

    d. The amount in dispute is rewarded to one of the parties.

chapter four

Enforcement of the NAR Code of Ethics

Learning Objectives

Upon completion of this chapter, you will be able to

- outline the procedures for processing ethics complaints and requests for arbitration along with recommended sanctions for persons found in violation of the NAR Code of Ethics;

- discuss actual case interpretations for an alleged violation of Articles dealing with Duties to Clients and Customers; and

- discuss actual case interpretations for an alleged violation of Articles dealing with Duties to the Public and Duties to REALTORS®.

■ Key Terms

domain name	letter of warning	public trust
due process	probation	sanction
expulsion	procuring cause	suspension
grievance committee	Professional Standards	
letter of reprimand	Hearing Panel	

◼ Introduction

All member boards or associations of the National Association of REALTORS® are required to both maintain and enforce the NAR Code of Ethics with respect to the business practices of all members. Any violation of the Code of Ethics where there is reason to believe the public trust may have been violated must also be reported to the state real estate licensing authority. "Public trust" is defined as demonstrated misappropriation of client or customer funds or property, willful discrimination, or fraud resulting in substantial economic harm. Acceptance of the Code of Ethics depends on fair, reasonable, and impartial enforcement and must never involve a sacrifice of the right to counsel or other procedural safeguards.

1. Learning Objective: Outline the procedures for processing ethics complaints and requests for arbitration along with recommended sanctions for persons found in violation of the NAR Code of Ethics.

◼ NAR Policies and Procedures

Enforcement of the Code of Ethics is handled at the local (and occasionally state) level by the grievance and professional standards committees. The number of members on each committee may vary, depending on the size of the board or association. All persons responsible for administering the enforcement procedures must have successfully completed training that matches the criteria established by NAR.

The *NAR Code of Ethics and Arbitration Manual* includes policies and procedures to be followed for both ethics and arbitration hearings, along with suggested forms to be used by the local or state board or association. The manual contains an Outline of Procedure for both an ethics hearing and an arbitration hearing. Adherence to these guidelines ensures due process for all parties involved. The manual is updated and reprinted annually.

Due Process

Basic due process rights include the

- ◼ right to know the nature of the complaint or arbitration request in advance,
- ◼ opportunity to prepare an adequate defense,
- ◼ right to call witnesses,
- ◼ right to present evidence or testimony,
- ◼ right to cross-examine witnesses called by the opposing side,
- ◼ right to have legal counsel present (there are some limitations on what actions such legal counsel may take), and
- ◼ right to a hearing panel made up of impartial peers (the complainant and respondent have an opportunity to review the names and refuse members of the proposed panel).

Role of the Grievance Committee

Any REALTOR® or member of the general public may file a complaint alleging that a REALTOR® has violated one or more of the articles of the Code of Ethics. Specific Standards of Practice can be cited as additional evidence but must refer to one of the 17 Articles. Once the complaint has been received by the local board or association, it is given to the grievance committee for review. This committee is made up of REALTOR® members and acts in a way similar to a grand jury.

In the case of an ethics complaint, the committee must decide if, assuming the facts presented are true, a violation might have occurred. If the committee decides there is no possible violation, the complaint will be dismissed. If the decision is made that there is a possible ethics violation, the complaint will be forwarded to a professional standards hearing panel. In a request for arbitration, the grievance committee must determine if arbitrable issues exist. If so, the request for arbitration will be sent to an arbitration hearing panel.

The Grievance Committee does not decide whether a violation has occurred and does not mediate or arbitrate business disputes. The committee may request a written response from the respondents, providing them with a written copy of the ethics complaint. The respondents are also reminded that failure to respond can result in a violation of Article 14 of the Code. Dismissals of ethics complaints and arbitration requests can be appealed to the Board of Directors of the association.

Professional Standards Hearing Panel

Members of the professional standards committee are chosen based on their experience in real estate practice and their ability to provide an unbiased and objective resolution. A professional standards hearing panel is made up of an uneven number of members selected from the Professional Standards Committee. In the hearing, both parties are given an opportunity to present their side of the case and may bring legal or REALTOR® counsel if they choose. After all the evidence has been presented, the parties are dismissed and the panel determines whether there has been a violation and, if so, what sanction should be given. According to NAR procedures, the standard of proof for alleged violations of the Code of Ethics must be clear, strong, and convincing evidence. Under no circumstances, does the Hearing Panel award money damages. The decision of the professional standards hearing panel may be appealed to the local board of directors.

Recommended Sanctions

No specific sanction or discipline for a particular violation is mandated by NAR because every case involves different circumstances. NAR does, however, publish recommended sanctions in the *Code of Ethics and Arbitration Manual*. After it has been determined that a violation has occurred, the panel may ask for the respondent's membership file. The sanction imposed may be influenced by the member's past track record of ethics violations. The discipline should be commensurate with the offense and should be progressive. Discipline for first-time violations should be educational but should be made more severe for repeated offenses.

The list of recommended sanctions includes

- a letter of warning with a copy placed in the member's file,
- a letter of reprimand with a copy placed in the member's file,
- a requirement to attend the ethics portion of the Board Indoctrination Course or other appropriate ethics course,
- an appropriate and reasonable fine not to exceed $15,000 (raised to $15,000 in 2013 for any violation occurring after January 1, 2014),
- probation for a stated period of time not to exceed one year,
- suspension from membership for not less than 30 days nor more than one year with automatic reinstatement if in good standing at end of suspension period; a board or association can choose to assess a penalty of between $5,000 and $15,000 in lieu of a suspension but only once during any three-year period,

- expulsion from membership for a stated period from one to three years with reinstatement only by application,
- suspension of MLS rights and privileges for no less than 30 days nor more than one year, and
- termination of MLS rights and privileges for a stated period from one to three years.

A board or association may also impose administrative processing fees up to $500 against a respondent found in violation of the Code of Ethics. This fee is in addition to any disciplinary sanction imposed. Administrative processing fees should be determined in advance and should be imposed as a matter of administrative routine.

The decision of the ethics hearing panel can be appealed to the Board of Directors but only on the basis of 1) misapplication or interpretation of the Article, 2) a lack of procedural due process, or 3) the discipline recommended by the hearing panel.

Arbitration Hearing Panel

As discussed in Chapter 3, Article 17 of the Code of Ethics requires members to resolve financial disputes through arbitration rather than through the courts. The arbitration hearing panel is composed of members of a local board or association. Based on criteria outlined in the *Code of Ethics and Arbitration Manual,* the hearing panel will determine which of the parties was the procuring cause of the successful transaction. The panel will then award the amount of money in dispute to that party. The NAR-required standard of proof for an arbitration decision is a preponderance of the evidence that determines which party was the procuring cause. The decision is not subject to appeal.

True/False Questions (Circle the correct answer)

1.   T   (F)   Specific sanctions are mandated by NAR for violation of one of the Articles of the Code of Ethics.

2.   (T)   F   The decision of either an ethics or an arbitration hearing panel can be appealed to the Board of Directors.

2. Learning Objective: Discuss actual case interpretations for an alleged violation of Articles dealing with Duties to Clients and Customers.

■ NAR Case Interpretations

The *NAR Code of Ethics and Arbitration Manual* contains numerous cases illustrating alleged violations of articles of the code. The interpretations are based on actual situations of alleged unethical conduct and include the decision reached by a hearing panel. The case interpretations in this chapter are taken from the 2014 edition of the manual and are representative of situations likely to occur in today's market. Although Standards of Practice may be used for further clarification, a violation must be alleged against one or more of the 17 articles. No specific sanctions or disciplines are suggested in these representative cases because the panel would have to take into consideration the people involved and the specifics of the case.

The number assigned to each case references the article involved (e.g., #1-28 refers to Article 1, case #28). At the conclusion of each case, you are asked how you would have voted if you were on the hearing panel. The actual hearing panel decisions are presented at the end of each case.

Case #1-28: Disclosure of Existence of Offers to Prospective Purchasers

(Adopted November 2002)

Seller S listed her home for sale with REALTOR® B. The property was priced reasonably and REALTOR® B was confident it would sell quickly. The listing agreement included the seller's authorization for publication in the MLS and authority to disclose the existence of offers to prospective purchasers.

Within days, REALTOR® B had shown the property to several prospective purchasers and one of them, Buyer Z, wrote a purchase offer at close to the asking price.

REALTOR® B called Seller S to make an appointment to present the offer. After hanging up with Seller S, REALTOR® B received another call, this time from REALTOR® A. REALTOR® A explained that he represented a buyer who was interested in making an offer on Seller S's property. REALTOR® A explained that while his buyer-client was quite interested in the property, price was also a concern. He asked REALTOR® B if there were other offers on the property, indicating that his buyer-client would likely make a higher offer if there were competing offers on the table. REALTOR® B responded telling REALTOR® A, "That's confidential information. Please tell your client to make his best offer."

Taken aback by REALTOR® B's comments, REALTOR® A shared them with his buyer-client, who chose not to make an offer and instead pursued other properties.

Buyer Z's offer was accepted by Seller S later that evening and, sometime later, the transaction closed.

Several months afterward, Seller S and REALTOR® A met at a social event. REALTOR® A related his conversation with REALTOR® B. Seller S asked REALTOR® A if he thought that REALTOR® A's buyer-client would have made an offer on Seller S's home absent REALTOR® B's refusal to disclose whether there were other offers pending. REALTOR® A responded that it was impossible to tell for certain, but his buyer-client had certainly not been favorably impressed by REALTOR® B's response to a seemingly routine question.

Seller S subsequently filed an ethics complaint against REALTOR® B, alleging violation of Article 1 as interpreted by Standard of Practice 1-15. He noted that he had clearly authorized REALTOR® B to disclose to buyers and cooperating brokers the existence of pending offers and that REALTOR® B's arbitrary refusal to share information he was authorized to share could have been the reason, or part of the reason, why REALTOR® A's client had chosen not to make an offer on Seller S's home.

REALTOR® B defended his actions indicating that while he agreed that he had an obligation to promote Seller S's interests, his obligation to REALTOR® A and to REALTOR® A's buyer-client was simply to be honest. He had not, in any fashion, misrepresented the availability of Seller S's property. Rather, he had simply told REALTOR® A to encourage his client to make his best offer. "I'm not required to turn every sale into an auction, am I?" he asked rhetorically. "I feel that I treated all parties honestly and fairly," he concluded.

You Be the Judge

1. If you were on the hearing panel, how would you vote? Do you believe that there was a violation of Article 1? *NO*

2. What convinced you to make your decision? *for buyer had no offer to make an offer*

3. Have you ever been in a similar situation? *NO*

If agreement exists to show you will do so

Hearing Panel Decision of Case #1-28

The hearing panel did not agree with REALTOR® B's reasoning, indicating that he had violated Article 1 as interpreted by Standard of Practice 1-15. They noted that Standard of Practice 1-15 requires REALTOR®, if they have the seller's approval, to divulge the existence of offers to purchase on listed property in response to inquiries from either potential buyers or from cooperating brokers. REALTOR® B had not met that obligation, and consequently, the hearing panel concluded that REALTOR® B had violated Article 1.

Case #1-25: Disclosure of Latent Defects

(Adopted November 2000)

REALTOR® A had listed Seller S's vintage home. Buyer B made a purchase offer that was contingent on a home inspection. The home inspection disclosed that the gas furnace was in need of replacement because unacceptable levels of carbon monoxide were being emitted.

Based on the home inspector's report, Buyer B chose not to proceed with the purchase.

REALTOR® A told Seller S that the condition of the furnace and the risk that it posed to the home's inhabitants would need to be disclosed to other potential purchasers. Seller S disagreed and instructed REALTOR® A not to say anything about the furnace to other potential purchasers. REALTOR® A replied that was an instruction he could not follow so REALTOR® A and Seller S terminated the listing agreement.

Three months later, REALTOR® A noticed that Seller S's home was back on the market and this time listed with REALTOR® Z. His curiosity piqued; REALTOR® A phoned REALTOR® Z and asked whether there was a new furnace in the home. "Why no," said REALTOR® Z. "Why do you ask?" REALTOR® A told REALTOR® Z about the home inspector's earlier findings and suggested that REALTOR® Z check with the seller to see if repairs had been made.

When REALTOR® Z raised the question with Seller S, Seller S was irate. "That's none of his business," said Seller S who became even angrier when REALTOR® Z advised him that potential purchasers would have to be told about the condition of the furnace since it posed a serious potential health risk.

Seller S filed an ethics complaint against REALTOR® A alleging that the physical condition of his property was confidential; that REALTOR® A had an ongoing duty to respect confidential information gained in the course of their relationship; and that REALTOR® A had breached Seller S's confidence by sharing information about the furnace with REALTOR® Z.

You Be the Judge

1. Do you think REALTOR® A was out of line in calling the new listing agent, REALTOR® Z? *No*

2. Was REALTOR® Z correct in telling the seller that the faulty furnace must be disclosed? *No*

3. Do sellers have the right to demand confidentiality on all matters concerning the property? *No*

4. Is a faulty furnace a "latent" defect or a "non-material" defect?

Hearing Panel Decision of Case #1-25

The hearing panel disagreed with Seller S's contentions. It noted that while REALTORS® do, in fact, have an obligation to preserve confidential information gained in the course of any relationship with the client, Standard of Practice 1-9 specifically provides that latent material defects are not considered "confidential information" under the Code of Ethics. Consequently, REALTOR® A's disclosure did not violate Article 1 of the Code of Ethics.

Case #2-7: Obligation to Determine Pertinent Facts

(Revised Case #9-13, May 1988. Transferred to Article 2 November 1994)

REALTOR® A, a homebuilder, showed one of his newly constructed houses to Buyer B. In discussion, the buyer observed that some kind of construction was beginning nearby. He asked REALTOR® A what it was. "I really don't know," said REALTOR® A, "but I believe it's the attractive new shopping center that has been planned for this area." Following the purchase, Buyer B learned that the new construction was to be a bottling plant and that the adjacent area was zoned industrial.

Charging that the proximity of the bottling plant would have caused him to reject the purchase of the home, Buyer B filed a complaint with the Board of REALTORS® charging REALTOR® A with unethical conduct for failing to disclose a pertinent fact. The grievance committee referred the complaint for a hearing before a hearing panel of the professional standards committee.

During the hearing, REALTOR® A's defense was that he had given an honest answer to Buyer B's question. At the time he had no positive knowledge about the new construction. He knew that other developers were planning an extensive shopping center in the general area and had simply ventured a guess. He pointed out, as indicated in Buyer B's testimony, that he had prefaced his response by saying he didn't know the answer to this question.

You Be the Judge

1. How would you vote? Do you believe that there was a violation of Article 2? *yes*

2. What convinced you to make your decision? *Should have checked*

3. Have you ever experienced a similar situation? *no for sure*

Hearing Panel Decision of Case #2-7

The hearing panel concluded that Buyer B's question had related to a pertinent fact; that REALTOR® A's competence required that REALTOR® A know the answer or, if he didn't know the answer, he should not have ventured a guess, but should have made a commitment to get the answer. The hearing panel also noted that although REALTOR® A had prefaced his response with "I don't know," he had nonetheless proceeded to respond and Buyer B was justified in relying on his response. REALTOR® A was found to have violated Article 2.

Case #2-19: Deceptive Information in MLS Compilations

(Adopted May 2004)

REALTOR® R searched the MLS compilation of current listings on behalf of his client, Dr. Z, who had recently completed his residency and was returning home to take a position on the staff of the community hospital. REALTOR® R's search returned several listings that satisfied Dr. Z's requirements, including a two-story residence listed with REALTOR® B that showed in the "Remarks" section of the property data form, "Pay your mortgage with rent from the apartment upstairs."

REALTOR® R attached the listings he'd identified to an email message that he sent to Dr. Z. A day later, REALTOR® R received a call from Dr. Z who told him there was something about REALTOR® B's listing that struck him as odd. "That house is in the neighborhood I grew up in," said Dr. Z, "I also remember our neighbors having a problem with the Building Department when they added a kitchen on the second floor so their grandmother could have her own apartment."

REALTOR® R assured Dr. Z that he would make the necessary inquiries and get back to him promptly. His call to the Building Department confirmed Dr. Z's suspicion that the home was zoned single family.

Feeling embarrassed and misled by REALTOR® B's apparent misrepresentation, REALTOR® R filed a complaint with the local association of REALTORS® alleging misrepresentation on the part of REALTOR® B for publishing inaccurate information in the MLS.

At the hearing convened to consider REALTOR® R's complaint, REALTOR® B acknowledged the seller had told him that the conversion had been made to code but without the necessary permits, and the apartment had never been rented. "I assumed the new owners could get a variance from the Building Department," he said.

You Be the Judge

1. What alerted REALTOR® R that there was a potential problem?
2. Does the fact that the apartment was never rented make any difference?
3. Does the fact that work was done according to code make any difference?
4. If REALTOR® B had not advertised the apartment as "income-producing" would it have made a difference?

Hearing Panel Decision of Case #2-19

The hearing panel did not agree with REALTOR® B's defense or rationale and concluded that showing a single-family home as having income-producing potential from an upstairs apartment which had never been rented was a misrepresentation that violated Article 2.

Case #3-10 Unresolved Contingencies

(Adopted May 2004)

REALTOR® A listed Seller S's house and placed the listing in the local association's MLS. Within a matter of days, REALTOR® X procured a full price offer from Buyer B. The offer specified that Buyer B's offer was contingent on the sale of Buyer B's current home. Seller S, anxious to sell, accepted Buyer B's offer but instructed REALTOR® A to continue marketing the property in hope that an offer that was not contingent on the sale of an existing home would be made.

A week later, REALTOR® Q, another cooperating broker working with an out-of-state transferee on a company-paid visit, contacted REALTOR® A to arrange a showing of Seller S's house for Buyer T. REALTOR® A contacted Seller S to advise him of the showing and then called REALTOR® Q to confirm that he and Buyer T could visit the property that evening. REALTOR® A said nothing about the previously-accepted purchase offer.

REALTOR® Q showed the property to Buyer T that evening and Buyer T signed a purchase offer for the full listed price. REALTOR® Q left the purchase offer at REALTOR® A's office. REALTOR® A informed Seller S about this second offer. At Seller S's instruction, Buyer B was informed of the second offer, and Buyer B waived the contingency in his purchase offer. REALTOR® A then informed REALTOR® Q that Seller S and Buyer B intended to close on their contract and the property was not available for purchase by Buyer T.

REALTOR® Q, believing that REALTOR® A's failure to disclose the existence of the accepted offer between Seller S and Buyer B at the time REALTOR® Q contacted REALTOR® A was in violation of Article 3 of the Code of Ethics, as interpreted by Standard of Practice 3-6, filed an ethics complaint with the association of REALTORS®.

At the hearing called to consider the complaint, REALTOR® A defended his actions noting that while Buyer B's offer had been accepted by Seller S, it had been contingent on the sale of Buyer B's current home. It was possible that Buyer B, if faced with a second offer, could have elected to withdraw from the contract. REALTOR® A argued that continuing to market the property and not making other brokers aware that the property was under contract promoted his client's best interests by continuing to attract potential buyers.

You Be the Judge

1. Do you agree with the decision of the panel?

2. What other argument could you have made in REALTOR® A's defense?

3. Does disclosure of a contingent offer hurt the marketability of a property?

Hearing Panel Decision of Case #3-10

The Hearing Panel disagreed with REALTOR® A's justification, pointing to the specific wording of Standard of Practice 3-6 which requires disclosure of accepted offers, including those with unresolved contingencies. REALTOR® A was found in violation of Article 3.

True/False Questions (Circle the correct answer)

1. (T) F   REALTOR® C makes it a practice to never disclose whether or not there are other offers to purchase on her listing. She is potentially in violation of Article 3.

2. (T) F   Based on Article 1, if a client requests that certain information be kept confidential, the REALTOR® must do so.

If legal

3. Learning Objective: Discuss actual case interpretations for an alleged violation of Articles dealing with Duties to the Public and Duties to REALTORS®.

Case #11-4: Disclosure of Limited Appraisal Experience

(Reaffirmed May 1988)

REALTOR® A was asked by Client B, an officer of a bank, to appraise an office building. In discussing the matter, REALTOR® A pointed out that, while he was an experienced appraiser, he had never appraised an office building. Client B expressed his confidence in REALTOR® A, based on years of satisfactory service in appraising residential property, and said that, notwithstanding REALTOR® A's lack of previous experience in appraising an office building, the bank wanted his judgment and asked him to accept the assignment to appraise the office building.

Accordingly, REALTOR® A undertook the assignment and completed his appraisal report. The report later came to the attention of REALTOR® C, who complained to the Board of REALTORS® that REALTOR® A had violated Article 11 of the Code of Ethics by taking an appraisal assignment outside the field of his experience without obtaining the assistance of an authority on office buildings.

At the hearing, Client B appeared as a witness for REALTOR® A and stated that the assignment had been given to REALTOR® A after he had disclosed his lack of previous experience in appraising office buildings and that the client was entirely satisfied by the manner in which REALTOR® A had completed his assignment.

You Be the Judge

1. How would you vote? Do you believe that there was a violation of Article 11?
2. What convinced you to make your decision?
3. What if REALTOR® C had testified that REALTOR® A's appraisal was entirely unrealistic and was much higher than the current market would support?

Hearing Panel Decision of Case #11-4

The hearing panel concluded that Client B's statement completely exonerated REALTOR® A of any violation of Article 11, since it was clear that he had disclosed his lack of previous experience in appraising the type of property in question and that he had been given the assignment after this disclosure was made to the client.

Case #12-22: Registration of Domain Names Based on Competitors' Firms' Names

(Adopted November 2008)

REALTOR® X was the principal broker of a small but growing real estate brokerage firm. REALTOR® X was constantly on the lookout for new and innovative ways to distinguish her firm from the competition and to increase its market share. Rather than simply relying on tried-and-true methods, REALTOR® X sought and often followed the advice of education, marketing, and technology consultants.

Based on the advice of her technology expert, REALTOR® X created and registered domain names for her firm, for the licensees affiliated with her, and for herself. A somewhat more troubling recommendation was that she register domain names mirroring the names of the real estate brokerage firms in her area with the largest market shares. When she questioned the consultant, he responded, "There's no reason why not. Everyone does it. It's just competition—and aggressive marketing."

When REALTOR® A tried to register a domain name for his firm ABC REALTORS®, he learned that domain name had already been registered by REALTOR® X. Doing further research, he learned the names of several other large companies in the area had also been registered as domain names by REALTOR® X. REALTOR® A filed an ethics complaint with the local association of REALTORS® charging REAL-TOR® X with violating Article 12 of the Code of Ethics as interpreted by Standard of Practice 12-12.

At the hearing, REALTOR® X defended her actions noting that Article 12 requires REALTORS® to "present a true picture in their advertising, marketing, and other representations." She pointed out that she had never used the registered domain name mirroring the name of REALTOR® A's firm, or those based on the names of other local firms. Since she had not used the domain names, she couldn't see how she had violated Article 12.

You Be the Judge

1. Do you think REALTOR® X had violated Article 12?
2. Do you have a domain name of your own?
3. Have you registered other domain names just in case you want them later?

Hearing Panel Decision of Case #12-22

The hearing panel did not agree with REALTOR® X's reasoning. The panel based its decision that REALTOR® X had violated Article 12 on the wording of Standard of Practice 12-12 which bars REALTORS® from registering URLs or domain names which, if used, would present less than a true picture. The panel also noted that the very act of registering a URL or domain name which, if used, would present an untrue picture is all that is required to violate Article 12, as interpreted by Standard of Practice 12-12.

Case #12-25: Advertising Role in Sales After Changing Firm Affiliation

(Adopted May 2009)

REALTOR® Q was a non-principal broker licensed with ABC REALTORS®. REALTOR® Q specialized in buyer representation. A prominent feature on her website carried the headline, "I sold these—and I can help you buy or sell, too!" Under the headline was a list of over a hundred street addresses of properties for which REALTOR® Q had found buyers.

For personal and professional reasons, REALTOR® Q chose to leave the ABC firm to affiliate with XYZ REALTOR®. As she transitioned to her new firm, REALTOR® Q was careful to disclose the name of her new firm in a readily apparent manner on her website. Her website also continued to display the list of properties she had found buyers for during her time with the ABC firm.

REALTOR® Q's parting with ABC had been amicable, so she was surprised to receive a complaint brought by her former principal broker, REALTOR® C, alleging a violation of Article 12, as interpreted by Standard of Practice 12-7, based on her website's display of sales made while REALTOR® Q had been affiliated with ABC.

At the hearing, REALTOR® C, the complainant, noted that Standard of Practice 12-7 provides, in part, "Only REALTORS® who participated in the transaction as the listing broker or cooperating broker (selling broker) may claim to have 'sold' the property. "It was ABC REALTORS®," REALTOR® C added, "that was the selling broker in these transactions, not our former sales associate REALTOR® Q. Her advertising our sales under the umbrella of her new firm, XYZ REALTORS®, is confusing at best, and potentially misleading to consumers who may get the impression the XYZ firm was involved in these transactions when that's not the case."

REALTOR® Q defended herself and her website, arguing the fact that she had found the buyers for each of the properties listed on her website was still true, and that the only thing that had changed was her firm affiliation. "If it was true when I was licensed with ABC, then it's still true even though I'm now licensed with XYZ," she reasoned.

You Be the Judge

1. How would you vote? Do you believe that there was a violation of Article 12?

2. What convinced you to make your decision?

3. Do you advertise on a website? Could you ever find yourself in the same situation as REALTOR® Q?

Hearing Panel Decision of Case #12-25

The hearing panel agreed that REALTOR® Q had, in fact, sold the properties, albeit while licensed with ABC. The ad, however, suggested that the sales were made while REALTOR® Q was licensed with XYZ, which was not the case. Consequently, REALTOR® Q was found in violation of Article 12.

Case #16-18: Assumed Consent for Direct Contact

(Reaffirmed Case #22-2 May 1988. Transferred to Article 3 November 1994. Transferred to Article 16 November 2001)

REALTOR® A, who held an exclusive listing of Client B's property, invited REALTOR® C to cooperate with him. When REALTOR® C, shortly thereafter, received an offer to purchase the property and took it to REALTOR® A, the latter took REALTOR® C with him to present the offer to Client B, and negotiations for the sale were started. The next day, REALTOR® C called on Client B alone, recommended that he accept the offer which was at less than the listed price, and Client B agreed. The contract was signed and the sale was made.

These facts were detailed in a complaint by REALTOR® A to the Board of REALTORS®, charging REALTOR® C with unethical conduct in violation of Article 16, having made his second contact with the client without his, REALTOR® A's, consent.

At the subsequent hearing, REALTOR® C defended his actions on the basis that since he had been invited to cooperate with REALTOR® A, and particularly since REALTOR® A had invited him to be present when his offer was presented to the seller, REALTOR® C had assumed that he had REALTOR® A's consent for subsequent direct contacts with Client B. He stated further that he had a good reason for going alone because in his first visit with the client, REALTOR® A had undertaken to present his, REALTOR® C's, offer without fully understanding it and had made an inept presentation. Questioning by members of the hearing panel revealed that there had been some important considerations that REALTOR® A had not understood or explained to the client.

You Be the Judge

yes

1. How would you vote? Do you believe that there was a violation of Article 16?

2. What convinced you to make your decision?

3. Is it common practice in your market area for the selling agent to meet with both the listing agent and the sellers for contract presentation?

Hearing Panel Decision of Case #16-18

The conclusion of the panel was that the consent of the listing broker required by Article 16, as interpreted by Standard of Practice 16-13, cannot be assumed, but must be expressed; and that REALTOR® C had violated Article 16 by negotiating directly with REALTOR® A's client without REALTOR® A's consent.

In 2012, NAR added three new cases to the Code of Ethics & Arbitration Manual based on Article 16, SOP 16-13. Following is the first of the three new cases.

Case #16-19: Continued Contact With Potential Seller Who Enters Into an Exclusive Listing With Another REALTOR®

After a decades-long career as a noted researcher and teacher, Professor Y decided to sell his home near the university campus in anticipation of his retirement to the northwoods. Having lived in the home for over 30 years and realizing that the proceeds from its sale would constitute a significant part of his retirement funds, Professor Y made appointments with several potential listing brokers, including REALTOR® P and REALTOR® Q. During each appointment, Professor Y asked extensive questions hoping to get a clear idea of his property's market value and each broker's proposed marketing strategies.

REALTOR® Q was familiar with Professor Y's home, having grown up on the same block and having gone to elementary and high school with Professor Y's children. Consequently, REALTOR® Q was not surprised when she received a call asking for a meeting to discuss a possible listing of Professor Y's home. The appointment had gone well and REALTOR® Q was confident she would get the listing. To her surprise, just three days later, the property came onto the market listed with REALTOR® P. REALTOR® Q was taken aback and spent considerable time pondering what she had done or said—or failed to do or say—that had led Professor Y to choose to list with REALTOR® P. Several times she was tempted to call Professor Y and ask why she hadn't been chosen, but she never made that call.

Several weeks later, Professor Y's son and daughter-in-law hosted a retirement party for Professor Y. Their friend REALTOR® Q was among the invited guests. At the party, Professor Y approached REALTOR® Q and, after exchanging pleasantries, commented, "You're probably wondering why I didn't list my home with you." "The thought crossed my mind," admitted REALTOR® Q, "but you made a good choice with REALTOR® P. I'm certain he'll do a fine job and get a fair price for you." Then, since Professor Y had raised the issue, REALTOR® Q asked, "Why didn't you give me the listing?" Professor Y explained that while he thought highly of REALTOR® Q, he had been very impressed with REALTOR® P's marketing strategies, and his choice was a business decision and not one influenced by friendships. REALTOR® Q accepted Professor Y's explanation and their conversation turned to other topics. A month later, REALTOR® Q was surprised to receive notice from the local association of REALTORS® advising she had been named in an ethics complaint alleging that her conversation with Professor Y, after Professor Y had listed his home with REALTOR® P, had violated Article 16 of the Code of Ethics.

At the hearing, REALTOR® Q had acknowledged she had been surprised and disappointed when Professor Y listed his home with REALTOR® P instead of with her. She also acknowledged she discussed Professor Y's choice of listing broker with him at the party. In her defense, she called Professor Y as a witness. Professor Y testified that he had in fact told REALTOR® P, his listing broker, about his conversation with REALTOR® Q, adding that he had no idea that REALTOR® P would file an ethics complaint. He also noted he—and not REALTOR® Q—had raised the subject of why he had chosen to list with REALTOR® P. "REALTOR® Q is a longtime friend of my family and I felt I owed her an explanation about why I listed with REALTOR® P instead of with her."

REALTOR® Q concluded her defense noting that while Standard of Practice 16-13 requires REALTORS® to conduct dealings related to exclusively listed property with the client's agent, there is an exception in cases where dealings are initiated by an exclusively-represented client. She pointed out that her conversation with Professor Y could fairly be characterized as a "dealing" related to Professor Y's exclusively listed home, and that her conversation with Professor Y, since it was initiated by Professor Y, did not violate Article 16 of the Code of Ethics.

You Be the Judge

1. Have you ever been in a similar situation?
2. Do you think REALTOR® Q acted improperly? *NO*
3. Was REALTOR® P justified in filing the complaint? *NO*
4. Was the Professor justified in choosing REALTOR® P? *yes*

Hearing Panel Decision of Case #16-19

The hearing panel concurred with REALTOR® Q's defense and found no violation of Article 16.

Case #17-1: Obligation to Submit to Arbitration

(Revised Case #14-2, May 1988. Transferred to Article 17 November 1994. Revised November 1995. Revised November 2001)

REALTOR® A and REALTOR® B had been engaged in a cooperative transaction that resulted in a dispute regarding entitlement to compensation. Rather than requesting arbitration before the Board of REALTORS®, REALTOR® A filed suit against REALTOR® B for payment of the compensation he felt REALTOR® B owed him. Upon receiving notification of the lawsuit, REALTOR® B filed a request for arbitration with the board, which was reviewed by the grievance committee and found to be a mandatory arbitration situation. REALTOR® A was advised of the grievance committee's decision but refused to withdraw from the lawsuit. Thereupon, REALTOR® B filed a complaint with the board charging a violation of Article 17 as supported by Standard of Practice 17-1.

REALTOR® A was directed to be present at a hearing on the complaint before the board of directors. Evidence that REALTOR® B had sought REALTOR® A's agreement to submit the dispute to arbitration was presented at the hearing. REALTOR® A defended his action in filing the suit and refusing to submit to arbitration by asserting that under laws of the state, the Board of REALTORS® had no authority to bar his access to the courts or to require him to arbitrate his dispute with REALTOR® B.

The board of directors concluded that REALTOR® A was correct as to his legal right and as to the board's lack of any right to prevent him from filing a suit. It was pointed out to REALTOR® A, however, that the Board of REALTORS® is a voluntary organization, whose members accept certain specified obligations with respect to their relations with other REALTORS®, and that if he wished to continue as a member of the board he would be obliged to adhere to the board's requirements as to arbitration.

You Be the Judge

1. How would you vote? Do you believe that there was a violation of Article 17?

2. What convinced you to make your decision?

3. Have you ever been involved in an arbitration dispute?

Hearing Panel Decision of Case #17-1

Because REALTOR® A would not withdraw the litigation, the board of directors concluded that REALTOR® A was in violation of Article 17 for refusing to arbitrate in a mandatory arbitration situation. However, it was noted that if REALTOR® A had filed litigation against REALTOR® B, and had REALTOR® B then requested arbitration with the grievance committee determining that an arbitrable issue of a mandatory nature existed, REALTOR® B might have successfully petitioned the court to remand the matter to the board for arbitration, and there would have been no finding of a violation of Article 17 since the board's arbitration process would have been ultimately complied with.

True/False Questions (Circle the correct answer)

1.   T   F   Article 16 is most directly connected with the Duties to Clients and Customers expressed in Articles 1 and 2.

2.   T   F   Based on Article 17, when a REALTOR® makes a request for arbitration they automatically give up any right to pursuing litigation.

> (Source: The preceding cases and answers have been reproduced with permission of the National Association of REALTORS®. Copyright 2014. All rights reserved. Select case interpretations reproduced from the *Code of Ethics and Arbitration Manual 2014*.)

■ Conclusion

A written Code of Ethics may provide inspiration and guidance to those pledged to follow it, but it is only relevant to the consumer if there is a system for enforcement of the tenets expressed in the code. If there are no sanctions for violating a code, there will always be members of an association who will disregard it and continue to practice in an unethical manner with little regard or respect for their responsibility to the public. It becomes the obligation of every member of the National Association of REALTORS® to not only support the code in their own actions, but to bring apparent unethical behavior on the part of their fellow REALTORS® to the attention of their local board or association.

■ Review Questions

1. Basic due process rights include all of the following *EXCEPT*
   a. right to call witnesses.
   b. right to be represented by legal counsel.
   c. right to know the nature of the complaint in advance.
   d. right to have a hearing panel made up of impartial peers.

2. The role of the Grievance Committee is similar to that of a
   a. courtroom jury.
   b. grand jury.
   c. mediator.
   d. judge.

3. An ethics Hearing Panel is empowered to do all of the following *EXCEPT*
   a. determine if a violation has occurred.
   b. decide upon an appropriate sanction.
   c. assign monetary damages.
   d. dismiss the case.

4. The recommended sanctions imposed for a violation of the Code of Ethics include all of the following *EXCEPT*
   a. a letter of reprimand.
   b. a requirement to attend an ethics course.
   c. a fine not to exceed $15,000.
   d. permanent expulsion from membership.

5. A professional standards hearing panel found REALTOR® Mary Jane to be in violation of Article 2. Because it is her first offense, they would be justified in issuing a sanction that she be suspended from membership for how long?
   a. 15 days
   b. 30 days
   c. 15 months
   d. Permanently

6. Any REALTOR® or member of the general public can file a complaint for a violation of
   a. only one Article of the Code at a time.
   b. any number of Articles at the same time.
   c. an individual Standard of Practice.
   d. multiple Standards of Practice.

7. REALTOR® C has buyer clients interested in REALTOR® F's listing. When she called to ask if there were other offers, REALTOR® F refused to give her this information. His action may be found to be a violation of
   a. Article 1.
   b. Article 2.
   c. Article 3.
   d. no violation.

8. While showing REALTOR® M's listing, REALTOR® T asked her what future zoning was planned for the property located adjacent to her listing. REALTOR® M has heard a rumor that it is to be changed to commercial. She should
   a. refuse to answer the question.
   b. divulge that information to Thomas.
   c. tell Thomas that she does not know.
   d. include that information in the listing brochure.

9. Article 2 of the Code of Ethics deals primarily with the disclosure of
   a. other offers to purchase.
   b. pertinent facts related to the transaction.
   c. accepted contingent offers.
   d. zoning restrictions.

10. Article 3 of the Code of Ethics requires disclosure of all
    a. accepted offers.
    b. non-contingent accepted offers.
    c. accepted offers except ones contingent on sale of other property.
    d. accepted offers with earnest money deposits.

11. Despite his lack of experience in land sales, REALTOR® William proceeded to act as a buyer agent for his client who wished to buy a tract of land for a town house development. Six months after settlement, the client learned that the city master plan would never allow town houses to be built in that area. If the client files an ethics complaint against William, the grievance committee may decide there is a possible violation of
    a. Article 11.
    b. Article 15.
    c. Article 16.
    d. Article 17.

12. Article 12 of the Code of Ethics has always required REALTORS® to present a true picture in advertising. Most recently, new Standards of Practice have been added dealing with the use of

    a.   paid advertising.

    b.   bulk mailings into a neighborhood.

    c.   who may advertise "sold" properties.

    d.   domain names.

13. REALTOR® L has a ratified contract on REALTOR® J's listing. REALTOR® L's clients have now decided they would like to settle at an earlier date. In this circumstance, REALTOR® L should

    a.   call the sellers directly to request the change in date.

    b.   prepare and deliver an addendum to the contract to the sellers.

    c.   prepare an addendum and deliver it to the listing agent.

    d.   call the listing agent to inform him of the requested change.

14. Any contact by a REALTOR® with the client of another REALTOR® might be construed as a violation of Article 16 *EXCEPT*

    a.   in a case where the REALTOR® had represented that person in an earlier transaction.

    b.   in a case where the REALTOR® and the client were personal friends.

    c.   in a case where the contact is initiated by the other REALTOR®'s client.

    d.   in a case where the contact is initiated by the REALTOR® in an informal setting.

15. REALTOR® E and REALTOR® C are in dispute over which one of them was the procuring cause for the sale of a property. REALTOR® C has notified REALTOR® E that she intends to file suit against him. Which of the following statements is *NOT* true?

    a.   REALTOR® C is prohibited from filing suit against REALTOR® E.

    b.   REALTOR® C has the right to file a suit against REALTOR® E.

    c.   Both REALTOR® C and REALTOR® E are obligated by Article 17 to submit to arbitration.

    d.   REALTOR® E could request the court to remand the case back to the Board of REALTORS® for arbitration.

chapter five

Current Ethics Issues

Learning Objectives

Upon completing this chapter, you will be able to

■ describe aggressive business practices that may affect the ethical behavior of agents under changing market conditions;

■ discuss and give examples of different real estate business models; and

■ review requirements of federal laws regarding communication and other business activities as they apply to real estate practice.

■ Key Terms

affiliated business arrangements	FACTA	one-stop shopping
backup contract	fee-for-service	pocket listing
CAN-SPAM	limited service representative	predatory lending
discount broker	MAP Rule	RESPA
escalation clause	National Do Not Call Registry	SAFE Act
ESL		subprime lending
		virtual office

■ Introduction

Many parts of the United States experienced a hot real estate market in the 1996 to 2006 decade. With a few exceptions, housing production and sales continued to rise throughout the country. The average home price increased steadily, reaching well over $200,000. The percentage of people owning their own homes rose to an all-time high of 69% thanks to low interest rates and special loan products that made mortgage loans more obtainable for more people. In many areas of the country, the supply of available housing was not able to keep up with the demand, which led to higher prices and a frenzied market as multiple potential homebuyers competed for the same properties.

1. Learning Objective: Describe aggressive business practices that may affect the ethical behavior of agents under changing market conditions.

■ Changing Times

Unfortunately, the extreme growth in the rate of homeownership in this country that occurred early in the first decade of the 21st century was primarily fueled by subprime lending. The subprime market exploded, increasing triple-fold in just a few years. As long as the overall housing market continued to climb, there was no problem. But as the value of property began to decrease starting in 2006, many borrowers were faced with sharp increases in their monthly payments when their subprime interest-only, hybrid, and pay-option ARMs began to reset. They were no longer able to make their payments nor were they able to refinance or even sell their homes.

The percentage of foreclosures began to double and even triple in many states and the mortgage loan industry went into a financial crisis unlike anything experienced in this country since the Great Depression. Because the number of foreclosed properties for sale affects the overall value of all homes in an area, many neighborhoods fell into a downward spiral that is still apparent in many parts of the country.

The government, the non-profits, and the mortgage lenders all began to scramble to work on special programs to try to help desperate homeowners save their homes. Ethics became an important issue when a lender either falsely represented the status of the subprime loan or forced a borrower into a subprime loan when it would have been possible for the borrower to have qualified for a standard loan with a little more effort on the part of the loan originator. A further ethical issue was when loan originators provided consumers with mortgage loans knowing full well that they would never be able to make the payments. These "junk" loans were then sold in packages on Wall Street further accelerating the financial crisis starting in 2007.

By 2010, most of the subprime lenders were either out of business or filing for bankruptcy. Fannie Mae and Freddie Mac remained under the control of the Federal Housing Finance Agency and yet another round of adjustable-rate mortgages began to reset driving even more people into potential foreclosure. Short sales became the buzz word as lenders were forced to accept that some return was better than no return. Despite a stagnant economy, the overall real estate market began to make a slow recovery in some parts of the country. Tightened qualifying standards made it more difficult to obtain a mortgage loan, but prices remained low and for those who were able to qualify, bargains were to be had. The competition for foreclosed properties began to increase. Unfortunately, desperate times lead to desperate measures and can result in unethical behavior on the part of lenders, borrowers, and other real estate professionals.

■ Unethical or Just Aggressive?

Although home prices range widely throughout the United States, the problem remains the same. In most towns and cities, there is a lack of housing that is affordable for those earning median income or less. The lack of supply in the lower price range along with much tighter qualifying standards for obtaining a loan have made it very difficult for potential homebuyers to find an affordable home. Ironically, some of the same aggressive marketing techniques that came into play during the hot market are now being seen as potential buyers compete for low-priced foreclosure properties. The market value of all properties—not just those in foreclosure—have been drastically reduced, particularly in areas that had seen extraordinary leaps in values just a few years earlier. All of this leads to an extremely competitive marketplace with aggressive marketing and tactics that often verge on being unethical. The following issues may be prevalent in some areas of the country and unknown in others, but all are representative of situations where a question of ethical behavior on the part of the agent may arise.

Pocket Listings

Brokers love to sell their own listings; and in a market where listings are many, but sales are few, there is obviously a temptation to hold on to a prime listing and market it only within the firm rather than through the MLS. This is often referred to as a pocket listing. It is, of course, not unethical if the seller chooses to instruct the broker to market in this fashion. However, it hardly meets the standard of broker cooperation as suggested in Article 3 of the NAR Code of Ethics nor of the usual business practice in a particular real estate market. One further issue is that of agency—are the best interests of the seller client really being promoted and protected as required by Article 1, when the property is not exposed to a wider range of potential purchasers?

Example: An elderly woman who was a personal friend of the principal broker of ABC Realty decided to move to an assisted-living facility in a city near where her daughter lived. Her home was in good physical condition and in a prime location. She was satisfied to ask a moderately low price for the property since it was paid for long ago and her financial needs were well covered. Knowing this would be a listing that would sell almost as soon as the information hit the MLS, the broker decided to limit the marketing to his own company. Within two hours of the sign going up in the yard, there were three offers made. The broker felt that he had served the best interests of the client by making it possible for her to avoid the strain of multiple potential buyers touring the home while still obtaining the price and terms that she wanted. Other brokers in the community felt that this was not showing the cooperation expected under Article 3 of the Code of Ethics and also did not meet the terms of the local MLS.

No Offers Considered Until Next Tuesday

Anticipating multiple offers on a property, the listing agent might include in the MLS printout the instructions that offers will not be considered by the seller until a given date that might be two or three days away from the time the property appears in the MLS. The NAR Code of Ethics says all offers shall be presented "objectively and as quickly as possible" (Article 1, SOP 1-6). Buyer agents might claim it is unfair that their offers, submitted on day one, have to wait to compete with others at a later date. The listing agent will argue that it is in the best interests of the seller to wait to receive as many offers as possible, providing an opportunity to select the best offer based on the conditions of the offer and the qualifications of the buyer. Adding to the problem is the case of a foreclosed property or one where the lender has indicated a willingness to accept a short sale (i.e., accepting less than the amount due on the loan). In many cases, the offer must be submitted to the lender for approval, which can be a matter of days or even weeks.

Raising the Ante

A fairly new phenomenon that occurred with the rising market and is being seen again is the use of an escalation clause. Similar to a poker hand, the buyer says, "I'll call your offer and raise you x number of thousands." So much for the old myth that the first full price offer on the seller's terms *must* be accepted. In many markets today, the asking price only opens the bidding process. Complications arise when several of the multiple offers have escalation clauses. What happens when Buyer A says, "I'll go $2,000 over the highest bid," and Buyer B also says "I'll go $2,000 over the highest bid"?

Where does the bidding stop? To avoid this problem, the agent can include an escalation clause in the purchase offer that states a maximum amount that will be offered. Suppose there is only one bid for full price at $180,000 that contains an escalation clause with a cap of $200,000. Would it be ethical for the seller to counter back at the $200,000 even though there was no other offer? A clear violation of ethics would occur if the listing agent claimed there was another offer in order to push the price up to $200,000. The escalation clause can be a useful tool in the buyer agent's toolbox but should be handled carefully.

Multiple Offer Protocol

The first reaction of most sellers when told that there are eight simultaneous offers on their property would be, "That's great!" In fact, it is not always quite so great. Whenever there are multiple offers, it is necessary for the seller and the listing agent to establish a system whereby all of the offers may be presented objectively and fairly. In some areas of the country, buyer agents are accustomed to making their own presentations; in other places, all offers are conveyed through the listing agent. Having all presenting agents at the table with the seller at one time might provide a buyer's agent with an opportunity to gain information that could be used to the seller's disadvantage. If one or two of the buyer agents have their buyer clients sitting in the next room or just outside the office waiting to immediately increase their offer or sign off on any contingencies, this strategy could put the other agents at a disadvantage.

Normal procedure in many parts of the country is for selling agents to submit all offers to purchase to the listing agent who then makes the presentation to the seller. In a case of multiple offers, the agent then creates a chart or matrix showing all salient points—price, financing terms, contingencies, settlement date, and so on—which is presented to the seller for discussion. With the assistance of the listing agent, the seller can then make counteroffers. It is essential that one contract be named primary with others as backups. If two or more contracts were countered without being designated in priority and all were accepted, the seller could be in a position of selling the house twice—or more. This would create not just an ethical dilemma but a legal one.

Shopping the Contract

Whenever demand far outreaches the supply of properties for sale, something like an auction atmosphere is created. Buyer agents try everything possible to make their client's offer the most attractive. Listing agents try to obtain the very best offer for their clients—which is not necessarily the highest price offer.

Case Study #1—Shopping the Contract

On Thursday, Michael is listing a beautifully maintained single-family home in a popular section of town at an attractive price. He knows that there will be multiple offers as soon as it comes on the market. Anticipating this, he has entered the following notation in the MLS listing:

All contract offers submitted to listing agent by 9:00 PM Sunday to be reviewed by the seller on Monday.

By Sunday evening, there are eight offers on the table. Following Michael's advice, the sellers reject three of the offers where the buyers do not appear to be well qualified. Of the remaining five, the first one to be submitted offers full price with no contingencies; three offer full price with minor contingencies; and one has offered $10,000 above asking price, but the offer is contingent on the buyers selling their current home. Michael now plans to contact the agents on the first four contracts to see if they want to up the ante to match the highest offer made.

For Discussion

1. Is it illegal for Michael to do this?

2. Is it unethical for Michael to do this?

3. Are the sellers committed to accepting the first full-price offer?

4. How should Michael and his seller clients respond to the multiple offers?

Case Study Questions

1. Withholding all offers of purchase until a designated time is without question a violation of
   a. the NAR Code of Ethics.
   b. state license law.
   c. common business practice in the area.
   d. none of the above.

2. A seller would be obligated to accept
   a. a full-price offer with contingencies.
   b. a full-price offer without contingencies.
   c. any offer that includes the asking price as listed in the MLS.
   d. no offer that is not satisfactory to the seller.

¿Habla Español?

One of the fastest growing groups of first-time buyers are immigrants to this country. The typical profile of the immigrant buyer is that of a married couple in their mid-30s to 40s with several children. In most cases, they have ample cash for a down payment and closing but may lack a job or credit history. Real estate brokers and lenders have to learn to accept alternative forms of qualifying standards to meet the needs of this particular group. Another problem occurs when the prospective purchasers do not understand English. It is natural for anyone entering into a major financial obligation to feel more comfortable working with those who speak their language and understand their particular culture. Unfortunately, the language barrier has sometimes led to a gross violation of ethical behavior by some real estate professionals who tend to prey upon the lack of knowledge about real estate transactions in America.

Case Study #2—ESL Clients

Phi and Hoang Nguyen immigrated to the United States ten years ago but have remained in a predominantly Vietnamese center-city neighborhood, working for Phi's uncle in his dry cleaner shop and socializing with other members of the Vietnamese community. As their two children begin to reach school age, they decide they would like to move out of the city to a neighborhood with better schools and recreation facilities and where the children will become fluent in the English language. They have lived frugally since reaching this country and have saved almost $40,000 for a down payment. Knowing limited English, they were happy to find a Vietnamese real estate agent who referred them to a Vietnamese loan officer and a Vietnamese real estate attorney. This gave the Nguyens a high level of comfort in proceeding to find a new home. Of course they had to rely solely upon their agent to explain the involved process of finding a property, making an offer, obtaining a mortgage loan, and going to closing. Throughout the process, they were confident that everything was being handled in their best interests.

The problem began when they decided on a property listed by Sally of ABC Realty. Sally, who knew nothing of the Vietnamese culture, was shocked when Vinh, the Nguyens' agent, suggested that she should raise the listing price by $30,000 just so the Nguyens could feel they had made a good bargain in purchasing the home at the full asking price. She was even more dismayed when Vinh kept coming back to her to negotiate for additional things that had not been included in the original offer. Sally was also perturbed when she learned that they were obtaining a mortgage loan with a 9.5% interest rate for 15 years. In a going market of 6% interest, this seemed out of line, but she realized this was not really any of her business because the Nguyens were Vinh's clients. The final shock came at the settlement table when she noticed they were also paying six discount points on their 9.5%, 15-year loan. Although both Vinh and the settlement agent spoke English, they conducted the entire settlement in Vietnamese, effectively excluding Sally and the sellers from the whole process. The final straw was when Sally noticed that the HUD-1 settlement sheet showed a $2,000 credit from the sellers to the buyers to cover miscellaneous repairs. Nothing had ever been discussed about needed repairs—at least not in English and not in writing. Sally was ready to call off the entire settlement, but her sellers had already purchased another home and really needed to settle on this day in order to carry funds forward for their next settlement the following day. Her protests to both Vinh and the attorney were met with shrugs and comments that this was totally appropriate behavior in the buyers' bargaining type of culture and the sellers could take it or leave it. Feeling backed against the wall, the sellers agreed to settle but blamed Sally for not representing them adequately as their agent.

For Discussion

1. Was Sally acting in the best interests of her clients?

2. Was Vinh acting in the best interests of his clients?

3. What is the loan officer's role in this transaction?

4. What is the settlement attorney's role in this transaction?

Case Study Questions

1. As a result of this case, Sally could file for a violation of the NAR Code of Ethics against
   a. the Nguyens' agent, Vinh.
   b. the mortgage loan officer.
   c. the settlement agent.
   d. none of the above.

2. Purchasers who have difficulty understanding English should *ALWAYS*
   a. work with someone from their country.
   b. work with someone who speaks their language.
   c. work with someone who speaks their language but is also fluent in English and American real estate law.
   d. work with an English-speaking agent but hire a translator who speaks their language.

True/False Questions (Circle the correct answer)

1.   T   F   Broker Martin has just taken a listing that he knows will sell very quickly. If he markets it only through his own agents and does not submit it to his local MLS, as instructed by his sellers, he will *NOT* be violating the NAR Code of Ethics.

2.   T   F   Jane has received six offers on her listing. She should advise her sellers to counter all six of them at the highest price offered.

2. Learning Objective: Discuss and give examples of different real estate business models.

■ Different Real Estate Business Models

Changes in the current real estate market are not limited to the interaction between agents and clients. There are also significant changes in the makeup of individual brokerage firms, both within the firm itself and in the type of business conducted. Sherman Antitrust law prevents anyone from telling a competitor what they must charge or from taking any action that could be construed as restraint of trade. If other members of the brokerage community should attempt to boycott or bad-mouth these different types of brokerage business models, they would be acting both unethically and illegally.

The A Team

Top producer advertisements at the end of the year may show what seem to be impossible numbers for total production—"$150 Million in Sales" or "600 Units Sold." In all likelihood, this agent is actually head of a team of agents and/or administrative assistants. Top listing agents often bring on a buyer agent or two to work with their buying clients. Personal assistants, both licensed and unlicensed (requirements vary by state law), may take care of showing property, holding open houses, meeting with inspectors, tracking paperwork, and all the myriad details involved in real estate transactions. Depending on state license law, sometimes this team of agents is actually a licensed entity under the greater umbrella of a large brokerage firm. The ethical question becomes whether it's fair for one agent to get the credit for four or five agents' work competing against an agent who chooses to work as a sole entity with no more than an administrative assistant. Local boards or associations determine the criteria for "Million Dollar Club," "Top

Producer Awards," and so on and have to develop policies to cover the dollar amounts involved and how agents may properly advertise themselves. For example, if Johnny advertises that he is the number one sales agent in his city, is it based on the dollar production, the number of units sold, or the accumulated production of Johnny and the three members of his A Team?

Is Bigger Better?

There are numerous mergers, affiliations, and direct buyouts occurring every day that create megafirms. There may be 80 to 100 agents affiliated with an office with one or two managing brokers. The use of computers, cell phones, and other quick means of communication make it unnecessary for all agents to work from a desk located within an office building. The opposite trend is towards the small independent firm that is geared towards a particular niche market (e.g., a firm that specializes in working with a particular ethnic clientele). (Caution here: the company policies must conform to all fair housing and Article 10 provisions against discrimination.)

The Virtual Office

The quantum leaps in technology have made tremendous changes in the way many real estate agents conduct their daily business. Social media like Facebook and Twitter make instant communication with a whole address book of clients (and potential clients) possible. Individual blogs on the internet have replaced the popular mailed newsletter for many up-and-coming real estate professionals. Blast emails make it possible for the broker to reach all affiliated agents instantly. Each year, the NAR magazine features the top "30 under 30" agents. They are innovative, creative, and full of clever new ideas—as well as extremely successful!

The benefits of high-technology have almost made it possible to operate a brokerage firm in a completely different style from the old standard of a large office space with multiple desks, phones, computers, and copiers. State laws may vary as to the exact responsibilities of a principal broker, but in most cases, as long as the broker is available to review and discuss documents and provide adequate training, then their job responsibilities have been met.

Discount Brokers

Any listing broker or buyer broker has the right to offer a discount to a client, although not to the other party to the transaction who is a customer. Offering a discount to a customer might be construed as a conflict of interest because the agent only represents the client, not the customer. A discount broker may offer the same services as a more traditional brokerage firm but at a discount for certain clients or under special circumstances (e.g., attempting to get started in a new market area, contributing to a charity, or supporting a local school or corporate office).

Fee-for-Service

Under the fee-for-services program, sellers can select which services they want from a menu that includes submission to an MLS, newspaper or magazine advertising, holding open houses, review of contracts, and so on. A set fee accompanies each service. This option might appeal to an experienced homeowner who has sold many houses in the past and does not feel a need for all of the services offered by a traditional listing broker. Buyer agents can also offer a fee-for-service menu.

Helping the Owner

There are several franchise brokerage firms that are directed at "for sale by owners" (FSBOs), offering limited services for a set fee. This type of firm might also use a fee-for-services menu or offer various sets of services for a specified amount. In a market where homes are selling quickly, this concept is popular with sellers who are hesitant to attempt to sell entirely on their own but do not feel the need for a full-service broker.

Limited Service Agents or Representatives

Some states have adopted a separate category of agent where a limited menu of services is established. Similar to the concept of independent contractor where the agent is only obligated to perform those duties outlined in a contract between the broker and the client, the limited service representative must also outline the specific duties that are to be performed. This concept has caused some problems with listing agents who end up feeling that some of the duties that are usually handled by a buyer's agent are being dumped on them.

Unethical, Illegal, or What?

None of the programs described previously are unethical or illegal. The ethical question is more likely to be concerned with how existing brokers react to and treat these new business models (e.g., boycotting the new discount broker in town or verbally attacking anything other than the tried-and-true exclusive-right-to-sell with MLS support). A common complaint is when a broker offering limited service enters the listing in the MLS with directions for any cooperating broker to deal directly with the seller. Although ethical (but not legal in some states), this practice can be extremely annoying to the selling broker, who now feels he must provide all of the service normally handled by a listing agent for the cooperative brokerage compensation stated in the MLS printout. On the other hand, for the selling broker to refuse to show that listing there becomes an issue of unethical behavior and lack of agency responsibility to the buyer client. The buyer agent is pledged to do everything possible to find a property suitable for the buyer client—not one that satisfies the buyer agent.

True/False Questions (Circle the correct answer)

1.   T   F   The current trend throughout the country is the formation of large mega-broker type firms.

2.   T   F   Limited Service and Fee-for-Service are essentially the same approach to representation.

3. Learning Objective: Review requirements of federal laws regarding communication and other business activities as they apply to real estate practice.

■ But It's the Law

Conforming to the laws of the land, state real estate law, and state regulatory real estate board or commission rules and regulations has always been part of the business practice of the real estate professional. Some federal legislation has made it more difficult to prospect for new business. In this case, it might still be ethical, but it is no longer legal.

Don't Call Me

Cold calling into a specific neighborhood or to numbers selected at random from the directory has been a prospecting tool for decades. Praised by some as the way they got off to a successful start in the business and cursed by many who dreaded the broker-mandated cold-calling nights at the office, cold calling per se has met its match.

As of October 1, 2003, a combination of laws from both the Federal Trade Commission (FTC) and the Federal Communications Commission (FCC) made it possible for consumers to stop receiving uninvited telemarketing calls from either in or out of state. All the consumer has to do is register either by phone (1-888-382-1222) or online (www.donotcall.gov) on the National Do Not Call Registry. Both land lines and cell phones can be registered. The law applies to any plan, program, or campaign to sell goods or services. This law effectively forbids real estate agents from making prospecting calls to anyone who is on this list. Exceptions would be someone with whom the agent has an existing business relationship, defined as 18 months after a business transaction and up to three months after a consumer inquiry or application. Even though making a general telephone canvass is not unethical (Article 16, SOP 16-2) and making general calls is not illegal, calling anyone on the National Do Not Call Registry *is* breaking the law.

As of January 1, 2005, a broker is required to search the register every 31 days to be sure that no one on the list is being called. With a potential fine of $16,000 for each violation, many brokers have issued a do-not-call policy for their offices eliminating any type of cold calling. The NAR Field Guide to Do-Not-Call and Do-Not-Fax contains additional information on how to develop a company policy to ensure compliance with the law.

The National Association of REALTORS® has taken a position with regard to calling a For Sale By Owner (FSBO). NAR says that as long as the call is made to discuss a potential purchaser's interest in the property and does not in any way solicit the listing, it should meet the guidelines of both law and ethics.

You've Got Mail!

Almost anyone with internet email service complains of the number of unsolicited junk mail messages that come through daily. McAfee, AOL, Norton, and others offer their customers antispam blockage, which limits incoming messages to those already in the subscriber's address box. The Controlling the Assault of Non-Solicited Pornography and Marketing (CAN-SPAM) Act of 2003 requires all unsolicited commercial email messages to be labeled and to include opt-out instructions and the sender's physical address. It also prohibits the use of deceptive subject lines and false headers. A do-not-email registry similar to the do-not-call registry was considered but dropped when it was decided that technical problems would make such a registry impossible in practice. Each violation of the CAN-SPAM Act is subject to a $16,000 fine.

General Mailings

Unethical? No. General mailings for solicitation of prospects is allowed in Article 16, SOP 16-2 of the Code of Ethics. Illegal? Possibly. Important provisions of the CAN-SPAM Act for real estate professionals to keep in mind are that all commercial messages must include

- a legitimate return email and physical postal address,
- a clear and conspicuous notice of the ability to opt-out (i.e., decline to receive further messages),
- opt-out mechanism active for at least 30 days after transmission, and
- clear and conspicuous notice that the message is an advertisement or solicitation.

The act does not apply to purely informational messages, such as t[...] association, or to transactional or relationship messages, defined in t[...] ongoing transaction between a business and a customer. For example, a [...] to a client regarding details of an ongoing transaction or related to the agen[...] resentation of the client is acceptable.

The instantaneous messaging and quick turnaround of information is very val[...] able in real estate practice today. Proper use of email for both sending and receiving can ensure that this tremendous asset remains a valuable tool and not an undesirable nuisance.

To Fax or Not to Fax

Like unwanted calls and emails, unwanted faxed messages waste paper, tie up machines, and are generally annoying to the receiver. On July 9, 2005, the Junk Fax Prevention Act was signed into law, making unsolicited fax messages illegal. The act does allow businesses to maintain contact with their established customers and clients through the use of fax. No-cost opt-out provisions must be provided. Prospecting agents are reminded that they must also be aware of any state laws regarding the use of fax messages.

I'll Never Tell

Maintaining the confidentiality of a client has always been a strong tenet of the NAR Code of Ethics. In Article 1, Standard of Practice 1-9 extends the obligation of the REALTOR® to preserve confidential information even beyond termination of the relationship. In a few states, the legal requirement for confidentiality ends upon termination of the agreement. NAR's position illustrates how ethics may actually go beyond the letter of the law.

FACTA

New federal legislation has carried the need for confidentiality one step further. In an effort to lessen the amount of identity theft, the Fair and Accurate Credit Transaction Act (FACTA) enacted June 1, 2005, now requires all companies or individuals who deal with sensitive consumer information to destroy all such information prior to disposing of it. In most cases, state law requires real estate brokerages to maintain agency agreements and transaction files for a number of years before disposal. The FTC is responsible for enforcement of the rule and suggests that companies put policies into place immediately to help prevent identity theft. The act applies to any medium containing personal information, including paper, CDs, discs, or even hard drives. Penalties for noncompliance can be severe, including civil liability, class-action suit, and state and federal law enforcement action.

Options for real estate brokers, lenders, and others involved in real estate practice are to shred, burn, or pulverize all personal information about their clients before disposing of a file. It is suggested that a qualified destruction vendor be brought in to handle the disposal of all personal information. Vendors may be found through the National Association for Information Destruction, Inc. (NAID) at www.naidonline.org.

SAFE Act

Secure and Fair Enforcement Mortgage Licensing (SAFE) was part of the Housing and Economic Recovery Act of 2008. SAFE was designed to provide better protection for consumers by establishing minimum standards for the licensing and registration of state-licensed mortgage loan originators. There was originally confusion as to whether the Act would apply to real estate agents providing mortgage information to their clients. HUD's ruling is that brokers and agents are exempt from the Act unless they actually engage in the business of originating loans.

he Mortgage Acts and Practices (MAP) Advertising Rule that took effect in 'gust 2011 allows agents to provide a client with general information regarding .rtgage loans (rates, terms, etc.) but prohibits providing details about a specific loan product. For example, the distribution of rate sheets at a homebuyer seminar would not fall under the MAP Rule but reviewing all the documentation needed for preapproval of a specific loan product with a client would be questionable. Prequalification of a potential purchaser in order to determine the appropriate price range is okay, but a detailed conversation about the merits of a particular adjustable-rate mortgage offered by one lender is not.

It was hoped that greater regulation of mortgage loan originators would eliminate much of the predatory lending that had previously existed. In more recent years, the largest share of predatory practices has occurred with companies promising distressed homeowners that they would "save their home." In most cases, this was a scam operation that took money from people who could ill afford it in return for virtually no assistance in resolving their financial difficulties. There are actually several different government lending programs that provide an opportunity to lower the mortgage payment to something within the homeowners ability to pay. HOPE NOW is an alliance of housing counselors, mortgage lenders, and investors working together to create an organized plan to help homeowners stay in their homes—both legally and ethically. See www.HOPENOW.com.

The Role of the REALTOR®

No one expects the REALTOR® to be completely knowledgeable about mortgage financing, but it is part of the duty and responsibility of an agent to assist a client to locate a lender who will work with that borrower in an ethical and professional manner. Understanding both the benefits and the pitfalls of subprime lending could make the difference in successfully completing a transaction. Awareness of predatory lending tactics could save the client from making a big mistake. A good source for keeping up with the latest in lending legislation is the Center for Responsible Lending at www.responsiblelending.org.

■ Understanding RESPA—Old Dog, New Tricks?

The Real Estate Settlement Procedures Act (RESPA) has been in effect since 1974 to provide consumers with better disclosure of settlement costs and to eliminate kickbacks or referral fees that unnecessarily increase settlement costs. Since July 21, 2011, RESPA has been administered and enforced by the Consumer Financial Protection Bureau (CFPB). Formerly under the direction of the Department of Housing and Urban Development (HUD), the RESPA regulations have undergone revisions several times, including the changes to the Good Faith Estimate and HUD-1 Settlement Sheet that are now required. Some confusion remains as to which actions are, or are not, allowed under these regulations, especially relating to the anti-kickback provisions in Section 8 of RESPA. A list of the service providers subject to RESPA includes the following:

- Real estate brokers and agents
- Mortgage bankers and mortgage brokers
- Title companies and title agents
- Home warranty companies

- Hazard insurance agents
- Appraisers
- Flood insurance and tax service providers
- Home and pest inspectors
- Credit reporting agencies

(In 2012, the House passed legislation that would have exempted home warranty companies from RESPA regulation, but the bill was dropped by the Senate. The HUD interpretation of the law prohibits any fee being paid unless a specific service is provided.)

RESPA's Section 8 provision that prohibits a real estate broker or agent from receiving a "thing of value" for referring business to a settlement service provider (e.g., mortgage banker, broker, title company, or agent) is similar to Article 6 of the Code, which says that a REALTOR® "shall not accept any commission, rebate or profit on expenditures made for their client, without the client's knowledge and consent." That article goes on to say, "When recommending real estate products or services (e.g., homeowner's insurance, warranty programs, mortgage financing, title insurance, etc.), REALTORS® shall disclose . . . any financial benefits or fees, other than real estate referral fees, the REALTOR® or REALTOR®'s firm may receive as a direct result of such recommendation."

Exceptions to RESPA Rules

Full disclosure keeps it ethical, but staying legal is a little more complicated. RESPA also prohibits any splitting of fees unless the fee is for an actual service performed. There are a number of exceptions to the rule, however, that affect the day-to-day real estate business:

- **Promotional and educational activities**
  Mortgage bankers, mortgage brokers, title insurance companies, and title agents can provide normal promotional and educational activities as long as these activities do not defray expenses that the real estate broker/agent would otherwise have had to pay.

- **Payments in return for goods provided or services performed**
  A real estate broker/agent may provide goods, facilities, and services that are actual, necessary, and distinct from what they already provide and receive payment commensurate with the value of those goods and services. If the payment exceeds market value, the excess will be considered a kickback and a violation of RESPA. Payment must not be based on whether the services resulted in a successful transaction and must be a flat fee.

- **Affiliated business arrangement**
  Real estate brokers and agents are permitted to own an interest in a mortgage brokerage or title company as long as the relationship is disclosed and the customer is not obligated to use that company. No payments can be received other than those based on the ownership interest in the company, and they must not vary based on the volume of referrals.

A violation of the Section 8 anti-kickback, referral fees, and unearned fees provisions of RESPA is subject to both criminal and civil penalties. For more information on working within the RESPA guidelines, see www.realtor.org. All real estate professionals are also reminded to review their own state laws that might preclude some of the activities allowed by RESPA.

RESPA Do's and Don'ts

The following examples of what RESPA does and does not allow can be found on the REALTOR® website at www.realtor.org.

Examples of permissible activities and payments include the following:

- A title agent provides a food tray for an open house, posts a sign in a prominent location indicating that the event was sponsored by the title agent, and distributes brochures about its services.
- A mortgage lender sponsors an educational lunch for real estate agents where employees of the lender are invited to speak. However, if the mortgage lender subsidizes the costs of continuing legal education credits, this activity may be seen as defraying costs the agent would otherwise incur and may be characterized as an <u>unallowable referral fee.</u> *Violation of Respa*
- A title company hosts an event that various individuals, including real estate agents, will attend and posts a sign identifying the title company's contribution to the event in a prominent location for all attending to see and distributes brochures regarding the title company's services.
- A hazard insurance company provides notepads, pens, or other office materials reflecting the hazard insurance company's name.
- A mortgage brokerage sponsors the hole-in-one contest at a golf tournament and prominently displays a sign reflecting the brokerage's name and involvement in the tournament.
- A real estate agent and mortgage broker jointly advertise their services in a real estate magazine, provided that each individual pays a share of the costs in proportion with his or her prominence in the advertisement.
- A lender pays a real estate agent fair market value to rent a desk, copy machine, and phone line in the real estate agent's office for a loan officer to prequalify applicants.
- A title agent pays for dinner for a real estate agent during which business is discussed, provided that such dinners are not a regular or expected occurrence.

Examples of <u>prohibited activities and payments include the follow</u>ing:

- A title company hosts a monthly dinner and reception for real estate agents.
- A mortgage broker pays for a lock-box without including any information identifying the mortgage broker on the lock-box.
- A mortgage lender provides lunch at an open house but does not distribute brochures or display any marketing materials.
- A hazard insurance company hosts a "happy hour" and dinner outing for real estate agents.
- A home inspector pays for a real estate agent to go to dinner but does not attend the dinner.
- A title company makes a lump-sum payment toward a function hosted by the real estate agent but does not provide advertising materials or make a presentation at the function.
- A mortgage broker buys tickets to a sporting event for a real estate agent or pays for the real estate agent to play a round of golf.
- A title company sponsors a "get away" in a tropical location, during which only an hour or two is dedicated to education and the remainder of the event is directed toward recreation.
- A mortgage lender only pays a real estate agent for taking the loan application and collecting credit documents if the activity results in a loan.

■ On the Web

Using the computer to research any subject or interest has become so commonplace that even preschoolers can do it. Having a personal computer or laptop has become as much a requirement for going to school today as a pencil box was a couple of generations ago. It comes as no surprise that people interested in buying a home automatically turn to the internet to research what is available for sale, where the property is located, the asking price, and details about the property and the surrounding community. Surveys show that almost 75% of people looking for a new home use the internet at some point in their search. Savvy listing agents today make sure their listings appear on national websites like www.realtor.com or on franchise or individual company websites and always include a link to their own personal website.

In their enthusiasm to present the most impressive showing of listings, some agents have run into a potential ethics violation. NAR has determined that providing a link to other real estate websites containing advertisements for other agents' listings is not unethical. The problem occurs when an agent *copies* information on another agent's listing and includes it on a personal website without obtaining permission. This would be in blatant violation if the actual listing agent's name and company were not given. Even if this identifying information is included, there is still the question of whether or not permission was granted. A seller has authorized the listing broker to advertise and, at least theoretically, might not wish to have this listing advertised by a different agent or company. Standards of Practice 12-8 through 12-11 were all added in 2007 to provide guidance regarding alleged violations of Article 12 based on internet content. In 2008, SOP-12 and SOP-13 were added referring to the use of URLs, domain names, and the display of professional designations. Two case examples of alleged violations of Article 12 were given in Chapter 4.

True/False Questions (Circle the correct answer)

1. T   F   Julian is making calls seeking new listings in a resort area located ten miles from his town. He will *NOT* be affected by the National Do Not Call Registry because the calls are all made within the same state.

2. T   F   Michele and François are licensed appraisers in their state. Because they do not practice real estate, they will *NOT* be subject to RESPA regulations.

■ Conclusion

Market conditions change, interest rates fluctuate, the supply of available housing diminishes or increases, and real estate agents respond to hot and slow markets in different ways. Aggressive business practices may at first appear to be unethical. Changes in the basic real estate brokerage business model are viewed with suspicion. New government regulations interfere with traditional prospecting tools. Real estate professionals by nature are generally resistant to change, but change is inevitable and responsible members of the real estate community will make the effort to observe, study, and work to understand the ethical issues that are created in today's current marketplace.

■ Review Questions

1. Aggressive business practices that tend to appear in a hot market where demand exceeds supply include all of the following *EXCEPT*
   a. pocket listings.
   b. delayed presentation of offers.
   c. magazine advertising.
   d. escalation clauses.

2. Broker T has a new listing that he is sure will sell very quickly so he retains it within his own company and does not enter it into his local MLS. This is an example of
   a. a pocket listing.
   b. raising the ante.
   c. delayed presentation.
   d. shopping the contract.

3. The biggest potential problem with an escalation clause is that it
   a. takes longer to be ratified.
   b. may have no defined stopping point.
   c. is unfair to the seller.
   d. is unfair to the purchaser.

4. The *MOST* important duty for the listing agent at a multiple offer presentation is to
   a. limit the amount of time for each presentation.
   b. discourage the sellers from asking questions.
   c. be sure that only one offer is designated as primary.
   d. counter all offers at the highest price.

5. The *BEST* rationale for holding all offers to be presented at a future time and date would be that it
   a. gives the listing agent a chance to take time off.
   b. allows time for a better selection of offers for the seller.
   c. gives the first offer presented priority.
   d. makes the presentation easier for the seller.

6. Several brokers from the west side of town had a luncheon meeting and discussed boycotting the new discount broker who had just opened an office in that area. The brokers would be in violation of
   a. the Sherman Antitrust Act.
   b. RESPA regulations.
   c. the Federal Trade Commission.
   d. the REALTOR® Code of Ethics.

7. The biggest problem with having separate teams within a general brokerage firm is
   a. how to pay the different parties.
   b. who gets the credit for production.
   c. determining each job description.
   d. where to seat them in the office.

8. The type of representation that is *MOST* likely to cause problems with a cooperating broker is
   a. the mega-broker.
   b. small-niche market broker.
   c. limited representative.
   d. fee-for-service.

9. Broker Bob is free to offer a discount on his regular brokerage services to any of the following *EXCEPT*
   a. clients in a new market area.
   b. clients belonging to a particular charity group.
   c. a purchaser of Broker Bob's listing.
   d. a seller of Broker Bob's listing.

10. Typical characteristics of a virtual office could be all of the following *EXCEPT*
    a. use of blast email.
    b. social media like Facebook and Twitter.
    c. floor duty schedule.
    d. individual agent or company blogs.

11. All of the following statements regarding the Do Not Call Registry are true *EXCEPT*
    a. the law applies to all calls made either within the state or out of state.
    b. the fine for each violation is $16,000.
    c. an agent is allowed to call all former clients.
    d. many brokers no longer allow "cold-calling nights" as a means of prospecting.

12. The requirement to destroy all sensitive consumer information is part of
    a. CAN-SPAM.
    b. RESPA.
    c. FACTA.
    d. MAP Rule.

13. The CAN-SPAM Act is an attempt to reduce the
    a. number of unsolicited phone calls.
    b. number of unsolicited emails.
    c. number of unsolicited fax messages.
    d. number of cans of SPAM sold overseas annually.

14. All of the following are permissible activities according to RESPA *EXCEPT*
    a. a title agent providing a food tray for an open house as part of a joint marketing plan.
    b. a mortgage lender subsidizing the cost of continuing education credits.
    c. a home inspection company sponsoring an association golf tournament distributing company brochures.
    d. a real estate agent and a mortgage broker jointly advertising services.

15. The purpose behind the creation of the SAFE Act was to
    a. regulate all mortgage loan originators.
    b. develop new loan products.
    c. protect the best interests of the consumer.
    d. eliminate subprime lending.

6

Making Ethical Decisions

Learning Objectives

Upon completing this chapter, you will be able to

■ discuss suggested tests for making ethical decisions including consideration of potential conflict of interest;

■ identify four paradigms of right versus right in ethical dilemmas; and

■ apply different principles of ethical decision making to case studies.

■ Key Terms

actual conflict of interest	Kidder's paradigms	potential conflict of interest
care-based principle	moral courage	
ends-based principle	moral mentor	rule-based principle
ethical dilemma		Standards of Conduct (the Golden Rule)

■ Introduction

Some present-day philosophers claim that behaving in an ethical manner is actually very easy to do as long as you always go by the Golden Rule: "Do unto others as you would have them do unto you." But suppose what you would like to have "done unto you" is not actually the most ethical solution to the problem. Others have proposed a Platinum Rule: "Do unto others as they would like to be done unto." Again, the way they would like to see the problem resolved is not necessarily the most ethical approach.

1. Learning Objective: Discuss suggested tests for making ethical decisions including consideration of potential conflict of interest.

■ Self-Testing for Ethical Decisions

Whenever faced with making an ethical decision, the first step is to take a good look at yourself. Start by answering the questions presented as part of Tom Morris's Six Tests of Ethical Action.

Six Tests of Ethical Action

Tom Morris, Chairman of the Morris Institute for Human Values, is a philosopher/consultant to large businesses such as Coca-Cola, NBC Sports, the U.S. Air Force, Toyota, CITI Mortgage, and the National Association of REALTORS®. He is also author of numerous books, including *If Aristotle Ran General Motors: The New Soul of Business*. His latest bestseller is *If Harry Potter Ran General Electric: Leadership Wisdom from the World of the Wizards*. Tom Morris has been described as the happiest philosopher of our time.

In his writing, Morris suggests "Six Tests of Ethical Action." These are simple tests to use in evaluating your actions and provide grounding for your decisions, especially where monetary gain, status, or power is at stake. They are summarized as follows:

- *The publicity test.* "Would I want to see this action described on the front page of the local paper?"
- *The transparency test.* "Could I give a clear explanation for the action, including an honest and transparent account of my motives that would satisfy a fair and dispassionate moral judge?"
- *The moral mentor test.* "What would my moral mentor (a wise and good person you admire) do in this situation?"
- *The admired observer test.* "What would make my moral mentor proud of me in this situation?"
- *The man/woman in the mirror test.* "Will I be able to look at myself in the mirror and respect the person I see there?"
- *The Golden Rule test.* "Would I like to be on the receiving end of this action and its potential consequences?"

Help in Making Decisions

There's an old adage that says, "When in doubt—disclose!" The same principle applies to making an ethical decision: "When in doubt—seek help!" For members of professional associations like the National Association of REALTORS®, the Mortgage Bankers Association, or the Appraisal Institute, there is a written code of ethics with examples and case studies that might apply to the current dilemma. For all licensees, there are state laws; regulatory board or commission rules and regulations; and in many cases, published standards of conduct. Although the people involved in today's ethical dilemma might think that this is a once-in-a-lifetime occurrence, in all likelihood this, or something very similar, has happened before. The vast bank of experience of other professionals can be a tremendous source of help for one struggling with making an ethical decision. Always being careful to protect the identity of the individuals involved, a professional may describe and discuss a situation with other professionals in the field. There are probably as many solutions as there are problems, but careful study of the situation, the decision, and the results from previous cases can often provide guidance.

The bottom line is, "Can I make a fair and unbiased decision that I am willing to live with?" If not, perhaps the decision should be made by someone else. If there is even the slightest hint that there could be a perceived conflict of interest, the problem should be turned over to someone else.

■ Real Estate Conflict of Interest—Actual or Perceived?

One area of real estate practice that has the potential for conflict of interest is dual agency. As long as no problems occur during the transaction, dual agency generally can be handled smoothly. Unfortunately, not many real estate transactions take place with no problems. The ethical dilemma arises when one of the parties feels that the agent has acted in such a way as to create a conflict of interest by showing preference to the other party to the transaction. For example, the buyers feel that the agent did not adequately disclose a severe drainage problem in the yard because the agent was protecting the best interests of the seller. Here is another example. The sellers are disturbed because the agent did not disclose that the buyers had credit problems, which is now causing a delay in getting to settlement. In either example, one side thinks the agent was favoring the other side. At this point, it does not really matter whether there is an actual conflict of interest or not—the effect is the same. To the consumer, perception is reality.

Avoiding Potential Conflict of Interest

In these situations, in addition to considering the questions in the six steps for ethical action consider the following:

■ Can you make the same unbiased, independent judgment that would be expected from anyone else in your position?

■ Is there anything about this situation that might make someone question your ability to make an independent decision?

■ Is there any element of personal interest in the outcome of the decision that could lead someone to think you had a conflict of interest?

■ Would you have any difficulty in defending your decision?

True/False Questions (Circle the correct answer)

1.   T   F   As long as the Golden Rule is followed, a real estate professional will always have the correct approach to ethical behavior.

2.   T   F   If you frequently review the NAR Code of Ethics, read all of the articles on the Institute for Global Ethics website, and attend every course on ethics offered by your local association, you may be confident of always making the right ethical decision.

2. Learning Objective: Identify four paradigms of right versus right in ethical dilemmas.

■ Right Versus Wrong or Right Versus Right?

The answer to this question is never as easy as it would appear on the surface. Certainly killing another person is wrong—but what about war, certain police actions, or defense of your home and family? Stealing is obviously a crime—but what about those who take food and water for their families during crises such as Hurricane Katrina? The question becomes what is the "more right" or the "less wrong"?

The Paradigms

Rushworth Kidder, in his book *How Good People Make Tough Choices* (Simon & Schuster, 1996), outlines four paradigms where right is on both sides of the dilemma. Of course, not all ethical dilemmas fit neatly into one or the other of the paradigms; in some cases, there may be some elements of all four. It can be helpful, however, to approach the dilemma from the viewpoint of the paradigms. At the least, it may lead to active discussion. Two of the paradigms are illustrated by reviewing cases presented earlier in the book. In each case, there is right on both sides of the problem. There are no easy black-and-white answers to any of these illustrations. The outcome of each one will depend on the particular circumstances, the persons involved, and their motivation to do what is seen as the right thing.

Paradigm #1: Truth Versus Loyalty

In Chapter 2, Case Study #4—"Megan's Law," Gloria is torn between telling the *truth* about the released sex offender living in the neighborhood to the buyers (who are not her clients) and her *loyalty* to the sellers, who are her clients. Let's review the case:

Gloria met with Mr. and Mrs. Martinez to list their three-bedroom, split-level home in a popular neighborhood for people with young children due to the proximity of both an elementary school and a public park. In the course of the conversation with the Martinezes about their future plans, Gloria learned that the reason they wished to move is that they had learned that the 45-year-old son of an elderly couple who lived on their block had just been released from a 15-year prison sentence as a sex offender and was returning to the neighborhood to live with his parents. The Martinezes did not want to live so close to this person because they have two sons, ages 5 and 7.

Because this is not a physical feature of the house, there is no requirement in Gloria's state for such a disclosure to be made. Gloria listed the home at a reasonable price and anticipated that it should be a quick sale, hopefully to someone with their own buyer agent.

The next day, Gloria received a call from Jack and Susan. Jack was being transferred to this city in three weeks, and they were in town for the weekend to look at property. They saw the For Sale sign on their way out to breakfast and wanted to see the house immediately. Gloria met them at the house and they loved it. When they wanted to prepare an offer right there at the kitchen table, she explained that she worked for the seller and would not actually be representing them. Having bought and sold many homes in the past, they didn't care about representation—they just wanted to buy this house. In the process of writing up the offer, Gloria learned that they have six-year-old twin girls and are expecting another child in six months.

Gloria feels a moral obligation to protect the safety of the buyers' family but is also bound by both law and the NAR Code of Ethics to protect and promote the best interests of her client. Providing adverse information to the buyers could quite possibly cause the sale to fall through, which would be damaging to the sellers. Following the letter of the law as it applies to agency responsibility provides a simple answer—don't tell. But ethics often go beyond the letter of the law.

No one can argue that telling the truth is *right* nor can it be argued that following the law is *right*. This is our first example of "right versus right." What would you do in a similar situation?

Paradigm #2: Individual Versus Community

Let's take another look at Case Study #5 in Chapter 2—"How Much Must I Say?"

Katherine is the listing agent for a 50-acre residential tract of land that is currently under contract. The buyer is going through the due diligence period and knows that he will have to rezone the property to build zero-lot-line homes as part of a mixed-use project in order to gain city approval.

Across the street from the 50-acre tract is a 200-acre residential tract of lakefront property that has just gone under contract. This property was never openly listed, but Katherine happens to know that Lakeside Development, the buyer, plans to rezone it for a mixed-use project. The plans for this property include high-end homes along the lake, but no decision has been made for the interior portion.

Katherine also knows that Lakeside Development would like to try for higher-density zoning, but based on her own experience, she knows that the city is not likely to approve this request.

Katherine's dilemma is whether or not she needs to disclose to the buyers (who are unrepresented) of her 50-acre piece the potential development coming across the street. These buyers are from out of town and have no real source of information except for Katherine. Although both projects involve residential concepts, the mixed-use concept will eventually add a tremendous amount of housing and commercial construction in an area that has not seen much growth for a number of years. It is possible that knowledge of the potential 200-acre project could affect the financial evaluation of the 50-acre tract by the buyers. Thomas, the agent for the current buyer of that tract, has approached Katherine and asked her to see if the buyer of the 50-acre tract will be willing to collaborate with his buyer in obtaining city approval for the mixed-use rezoning.

To make the situation even more complicated, Katherine is acting as a buyer's agent for Stanley & Co., who has a backup contract on the 200-acre site. Katherine does not want to disclose her buyer-agent status with Stanley & Co. to Thomas, and she is not sure if collaborating on the rezoning process would be in the best interest of her seller client for the 50 acres. It seems that Katherine is the only one who knows all of the players involved and most of the proposed plans. She is concerned about being placed in a position of liability for not disclosing material facts, but she is also concerned about maintaining her responsibility to both her seller client and her buyer client.

This case illustrates a situation where an agent is torn between what is an easy short-term solution for an *individual* versus what may be the best option for several parties in the *community* in the future. Katherine's seller client has a 50-acre piece of land to sell and there are buyers who wish to buy it. On the surface, this might seem to be a no-brainer. It becomes complicated due to Katherine's awareness of the plans for the 200-acre mixed-use development across the street. The ethical dilemma is heightened by the fact that Katherine is also the buyer agent for a party with a backup contract on the 200-acre piece. How would the proposed rezoning affect the values of the property? Rezoning of the combined pieces of property might be the best solution for the greatest number of people, but should this take precedence over Katherine's responsibility to her current client who just wants to sell the 50 acres? This case illustrates not only the paradigm of Individual Versus Community but also Short-Term Versus Long-Term.

Paradigm #3: Short-Term Versus Long-Term

What appears to be a right decision for today might not be what would be considered right at a later point in time. Both the law and the NAR Code of Ethics are very clear that the real estate agent must not practice law. However, responsible agents do have a general knowledge of real estate law and should be prepared to refer their clients for legal counsel when a legal question arises. All prelicensing courses contain a chapter on ways to take ownership of a property, including a discussion of the difference between joint tenants with right of survivorship and tenants in common. Consider the ethical dilemma Martha faced in the following real-life situation (with names changed).

Martha is the listing agent for a town house owned by the Williams. The buyers are two young men in their late 20s who both serve in the Army reserves. At the closing, she notices the buyers are taking title to the property as joint tenants with rights of survivorship. While waiting for the attorney to arrive, Martha, her clients, the buyer's agent, and the buyers—Jack and Jimmy—sit around the anteroom chatting. Jack and Jimmy are happily discussing Jack's recent engagement with marriage plans for the following year. In the *short term*, the joint tenancy might be okay, but Martha wonders if once Jack is married, he would, in the event of his death, choose to have his interest in the town house convey to his wife rather than to Jimmy. Of course the Williams are her clients, not the buyers. Is the right action to recommend that the buyers discuss the *long-term* outcome of how they take title? Or should she just remain silent?

Martha decided to ask the question. The settlement was delayed while the attorney was brought in to explain the difference between joint tenancy and tenants in common. When the explanation was completed, the young men decided that tenants in common was a much better choice. The sellers were a little annoyed that the question of how to take title was not brought up prior to the time of settlement but waited patiently while the explanation was made. In the end, the sellers thanked Martha for raising the question. The Williams had met the young men when they were looking at the property and wanted what was best for Jack and Jimmy.

Paradigm #4: Justice Versus Mercy

There are cases where the right legal position is not always the right ethical one. Real estate agents who specialize in working with senior citizens could face the problem of what to do when one of the parties dies during the middle of the real estate transaction.

For example, Mr. and Mrs. Hamilton listed their Cleveland home with Miguel on October 1. The Hamiltons planned to move to Mount Dora, Florida, to a home they had been using for a winter residence for a number of years. A full-price offer with a November 15 settlement date was made by the Dillons on October 8 and accepted by the Hamiltons. Unfortunately, Mr. Hamilton suffered a massive heart attack on November 1 and died. The legal status of the Dillons is clear; they have a ratified contract for the purchase of the house. They definitely have the legal right to proceed with their purchase and *justice* will be served. However, Mrs. Hamilton confided to Miguel that she never really wanted to move to Florida. Her children and grandchildren are still located in the Cleveland area and she wants very badly to remain in her home of 40 years and stay close to her family. Miguel decides to appeal to the Dillons through their buyer agent, Dale. He asks Dale to ask the Dillons if they would consider showing *mercy* by voiding the contract, allowing Mrs. Hamilton to remain in her home.

The Dillons' response, of course, will be based not only on their humanitarian instincts but also on their own plans for moving. They could, as a matter of goodwill, allow the contract to be terminated. On the other hand, if they have sold their present home or their lease has been terminated, they may not have the luxury of time to allow for finding another place to live.

True/False Questions (Circle the correct answer)

1. T   F   In every ethical situation, there is a clear-cut sense of right versus wrong.

2. T   F   Regardless of the circumstances, a real estate professional should always strictly follow the rules and regulations.

3. Learning Objective: Apply different principles of ethical decision-making to case studies.

■ Principles for Decision Making

In Rushworth Kidder's book, *Moral Courage* (HarperCollins, 2005), he reminds us that merely determining into which paradigm an ethical dilemma may fall does not provide an answer to the dilemma. Ultimately, a decision must be made. Remembering that these are all cases of right versus right, there does not have to be one party who is wrong. After researching thousands of decisions made by participants in seminars sponsored by the Institute for Global Ethics, Kidder determined that the most commonly used principles for decision making fall into the following three categories:

■ *Ends-based* principle of utilitarianism, or doing what is the greatest good for the most people. It is primarily focused on arriving at a good outcome and is not so concerned with personal motivation or basic rules and standards.

■ *Rule-based* principle, which means just what it implies—following the established rules in all situations regardless of consequences. This principle is similar to the teachings of German philosopher Immanuel Kant who believed that everyone should always react in the same way for any given situation, regardless of circumstances.

■ *Care-based* principle, which can be simplified by saying that following the Golden Rule will always ensure that our actions are ethical. A basic tenet of both Christianity and Judaism, this principle relies on putting yourself in another's shoes and responding in the way that you would want to be treated.

Applying the Principles

In the example of Truth Versus Loyalty, Gloria could make a rules-based decision by saying nothing to the purchasers. An ends-based decision would require her to take into account what is best for all of the parties involved. Empathizing with the buyer and their young family would result in a care-based decision.

In the Individual Versus Community example, Katherine could continue with the sale of the 50-acre piece and consider that her rules-based decision was adequate. Trying to work out the best solution for the greatest number of persons potentially involved in this complicated transaction would require an ends-based decision. A care-based decision would be torn between Katherine's seller client and her buyer client.

A rules-based solution for Martha in the Short-Term Versus Long-Term example is easy—just sit there and be quiet. A care-based decision would require her to open the question of the best solution for the young men taking title to the property. An ends-based decision would be difficult to make without more information.

In the Justice Versus Mercy example, Miguel has no requirement to go beyond the rules-based decision to continue with the sale; however, a care-based decision would involve taking into account Mrs. Hamilton's feelings and trying to help her remain in her home. This is another case where an ends-based decision would be difficult to discover what exactly the best solution would be for all those involved.

Developing Moral Courage

In Kidder's book *Moral Courage*, he provides us with a checklist to follow in order to pursue the goal of achieving moral courage. These seven checkpoints seem to provide an appropriate closing for this study of everyday ethics in real estate.

Checkpoint #1—Assess the situation.   Is this a case that only requires physical courage or is moral courage needed?

Checkpoint #2—Scan for values.   What are the values involved in the case and how can I build on them?

Checkpoint #3—Stand for conscience.   Which of the principles involved need to be most strongly defended?

Checkpoint #4—Contemplate the dangers.   Are there risks or threats liable to occur?

Checkpoint #5—Endure the hardships.   Will I be able to endure the consequences of my actions?

Checkpoint #6—Avoid the pitfalls.   Can I remain strong against timidity and foolhardiness?

Checkpoint #7—Develop moral courage.   Is it possible to learn moral courage or is it simply an innate ability?

True/False Questions (Circle the correct answer)

1.   T   F   The ends-based principle of decision-making is based on the teachings of Immanuel Kant.

2.   T   F   Moral courage is an ideal that can be learned and developed to a higher level.

■ A Final Word

Will you always come up with the perfect solution? No. Will you always come up with the right solution? Possibly not. But if after careful study and thoughtful consideration, you reach a decision that you feel in your heart is fair, unbiased, and conforms to the best standards of ethical business practice, that is really the best that you can do. Learn to live with your decision and be ready for the next ethical challenge.

■ Review Questions

1. Tom Morris's "Six Tests of Ethical Action" include all of the following *EXCEPT*
   a. publicity test.
   b. moral mentor test.
   c. admired observer test.
   d. conflict of interest test.

2. When you ask yourself whether you want to see your action described on the front page of the local paper, you are using which of Tom Morris's "Six Tests of Ethical Action"?
   a. Publicity test
   b. Moral mentor test
   c. Admired observer test
   d. Man/woman in the mirror test

3. Jordene joined Jonathan's brokerage firm right out of real estate school. She has worked closely with him for six years and has always found him to be fair and honest in his dealings with the agents as well as with the general public. Jonathan could be described as
   a. a moral mentor.
   b. an admired observer.
   c. a man in the mirror.
   d. a Golden Ruler.

4. A conflict of interest issue is *MOST* likely to come up during
   a. single agency.
   b. dual agency.
   c. designated agency.
   d. subagency.

5. Broker Julia must resolve an ethical problem that has come up between Helene and Bill, two of her salespersons. Although Julia is a member of Helene's bridge club, she is still confident that she can make an unbiased, independent decision. Julia should
   a. proceed as the one to resolve the problem.
   b. ask Helene if she believes she will make an unbiased decision.
   c. ask Bill if he has any problem with her making the final decision.
   d. turn the decision making over to someone else.

6. Rushworth Kidder's four paradigms of right versus right include all of the following *EXCEPT*
   a. Truth Versus Loyalty.
   b. Individual Versus Community.
   c. Right Versus Wrong.
   d. Short-Term Versus Long-Term.

7. The case study where Gloria is torn between fully representing her client and what is best for a young family is an example of the paradigm of
   a. Truth Versus Loyalty.
   b. Individual Versus Community.
   c. Short-term Versus Long-term.
   d. Justice Versus Mercy.

8. The Individual Versus Community paradigm is often closely related to that of
   a. Truth Versus Loyalty.
   b. Short-term Versus Long-term.
   c. Justice Versus Mercy.
   d. Conflict Versus Interest.

9. A broker is trying to entice the number one listing agent in his community to join his office. If he decides to provide her with a private office and other benefits that are *NOT* available to his other agents, he may be facing the paradigm of
   a. Truth Versus Loyalty.
   b. Individual Versus Community.
   c. Short-term Versus Long-term.
   d. Justice Versus Mercy.

10. A broker has been directed by her home office to drop any agent in her branch who is not generating a minimum of 10 sales per year. She has to make a decision about one of her agents who has been with the company for 30 years but no longer does much production. She will be faced with the paradigm of
   a. Truth Versus Loyalty.
   b. Individual Versus Community.
   c. Short-term Versus Long-term.
   d. Justice Versus Mercy.

11. A broker has decided to make it a company policy that no agents may act as a dual agent when selling their own listings. Some of the agents are complaining about his decision, believing that they can give responsible service to both buyer and seller clients. But the broker believes this is the best decision for the company. This is an example of

    a. an ends-based principle of decision making.

    b. a rule-based principle of decision making.

    c. a care-based principle of decision making.

    d. none of these.

12. A broker has a policy that any agent who has more than three unexcused absences from sales meetings in a year will be fired. One of her new agents seems to have great potential as an agent but has three small children at home that often cause last-minute problems for her. She has just missed her fourth sales meeting. If Helen decides to give her another chance, she has based her decision on

    a. the ends-based principle.

    b. the rule-based principle.

    c. the care-based principle.

    d. Justice Versus Mercy.

13. Sally is a newly licensed agent who has joined Broker Jane's company. She has not been able to afford to pay the dues and other fees to join the local association of REALTORS® and receive a lockbox key. Her sister is very interested in buying a house just listed by fellow agent John. John is busy with another client and loans Sally his lockbox key so she can show the house. This is against the association rules regarding lockboxes. If Jane makes a rule-based principle decision, she will

    a. report Sally to the association.

    b. report John to the association.

    c. report both Sally and John to the association.

    d. let both of them go with a reprimand.

14. The paradigm of Justice Versus Mercy is *MOST* similar to the decision-making principle of

    a. the ends-based principle.

    b. the rule-based principle.

    c. the care-based principle.

    d. none of these.

15. Standing for conscience and enduring the hardships are part of Rushworth Kidder's seven-point checklist for developing

    a. physical courage.

    b. moral courage.

    c. right versus right paradigms.

    d. avoidance of conflict of interest.

Code of Ethics and Standards of Practice of the National Association of REALTORS®

[handwritten annotations in top margin: "SOP", "Standards of Practice", "What Art what # won't ask on Test / But focus on how you do your job"]

Code of Ethics and Standards of Practice
of the NATIONAL ASSOCIATION OF REALTORS®
Effective January 1, 2014

Where the word REALTORS® is used in this Code and Preamble, it shall be deemed to include REALTOR-ASSOCIATE®s.

While the Code of Ethics establishes obligations that may be higher than those mandated by law, in any instance where the Code of Ethics and the law conflict, the obligations of the law must take precedence.

Preamble

Under all is the land. Upon its wise utilization and widely allocated ownership depend the survival and growth of free institutions and of our civilization. REALTORS® should recognize that the interests of the nation and its citizens require the highest and best use of the land and the widest distribution of land ownership. They require the creation of adequate housing, the building of functioning cities, the development of productive industries and farms, and the preservation of a healthful environment.

Such interests impose obligations beyond those of ordinary commerce. They impose grave social responsibility and a patriotic duty to which REALTORS® should dedicate themselves, and for which they should be diligent in preparing themselves. REALTORS®, therefore, are zealous to maintain and improve the standards of their calling and share with their fellow REALTORS® a common responsibility for its integrity and honor.

In recognition and appreciation of their obligations to clients, customers, the public, and each other, REALTORS® continuously strive to become and remain informed on issues affecting real estate and, as knowledgeable professionals, they willingly share the fruit of their experience and study with others. They identify and take steps, through enforcement of this Code of Ethics and by assisting appropriate regulatory bodies, to eliminate practices which may damage the public or which might discredit or bring dishonor to the real estate profession. REALTORS® having direct personal knowledge of conduct that may violate the Code of Ethics involving misappropriation of client or customer funds or property, willful discrimination, or fraud resulting in substantial economic harm, bring such matters to the attention of the appropriate Board or Association of REALTORS®. (Amended 1/00)

Realizing that cooperation with other real estate professionals promotes the best interests of those who utilize their services, REALTORS® urge exclusive representation of clients; do not attempt to gain any unfair advantage over their competitors; and they refrain from making unsolicited comments about other practitioners. In instances where their opinion is sought, or where REALTORS® believe that comment is necessary, their opinion is offered in an objective, professional manner, uninfluenced by any personal motivation or potential advantage or gain.

The term REALTOR® has come to connote competency, fairness, and high integrity resulting from adherence to a lofty ideal of moral conduct in business relations. No inducement of profit and no instruction from clients ever can justify departure from this ideal.

In the interpretation of this obligation, REALTORS® can take no safer guide than that which has been handed down through the centuries, embodied in the Golden Rule, "Whatsoever ye would that others should do to you, do ye even so to them."

Accepting this standard as their own, REALTORS® pledge to observe its spirit in all of their activities whether conducted personally, through associates or others, or via technological means, and to conduct their business in accordance with the tenets set forth below. (Amended 1/07)

Duties to Clients and Customers

Article 1

When representing a buyer, seller, landlord, tenant, or other client as an agent, REALTORS® pledge themselves to protect and promote the interests of their client. This obligation to the client is primary, but it does not relieve REALTORS® of their obligation to treat all parties honestly. When serving a buyer, seller, landlord, tenant or other party in a non-agency capacity, REALTORS® remain obligated to treat all parties honestly. (Amended 1/01)

- **Standard of Practice 1-1**
  REALTORS®, when acting as principals in a real estate transaction, remain obligated by the duties imposed by the Code of Ethics. (Amended 1/93)

- **Standard of Practice 1-2**
  The duties imposed by the Code of Ethics encompass all real estate-related activities and transactions whether conducted in person, electronically, or through any other means.

  The duties the Code of Ethics imposes are applicable whether REALTORS® are acting as agents or in legally recognized non-agency capacities except that any duty imposed exclusively on agents by law or regulation shall not be imposed by this Code of Ethics on REALTORS® acting in non-agency capacities.

  As used in this Code of Ethics, "client" means the person(s) or entity(ies) with whom a REALTOR® or a REALTOR®'s firm has an agency or legally recognized non-agency relationship; "customer" means a party to a real estate transaction who receives information, services, or benefits but has no contractual relationship with the REALTOR® or the REALTOR®'s firm; "prospect" means a purchaser, seller, tenant, or landlord who is not subject to a representation relationship with the REALTOR® or REALTOR®'s firm; "agent" means a real estate licensee (including brokers and sales associates) acting in an agency relationship as defined by state law or regulation; and "broker" means a real estate licensee (including brokers and sales associates) acting as an agent or in a legally recognized non-agency capacity. (Adopted 1/95, Amended 1/07)

- **Standard of Practice 1-3**
  REALTORS®, in attempting to secure a listing, shall not deliberately mislead the owner as to market value.

- **Standard of Practice 1-4**
  REALTORS®, when seeking to become a buyer/tenant representative, shall not mislead buyers or tenants as to savings or other benefits that might be realized through use of the REALTOR®'s services. (Amended 1/93)

- **Standard of Practice 1-5**
  REALTORS® may represent the seller/landlord and buyer/tenant in the

NATIONAL
ASSOCIATION *of*
REALTORS®

same transaction only after full disclosure to and with informed consent of both parties. *(Adopted 1/93)*

· **Standard of Practice 1-6**

REALTORS® shall submit offers and counter-offers objectively and as quickly as possible. *(Adopted 1/93, Amended 1/95)*

· **Standard of Practice 1-7**

When acting as listing brokers, REALTORS® shall continue to submit to the seller/landlord all offers and counter-offers until closing or execution of a lease unless the seller/landlord has waived this obligation in writing. REALTORS® shall not be obligated to continue to market the property after an offer has been accepted by the seller/landlord. REALTORS® shall recommend that sellers/landlords obtain the advice of legal counsel prior to acceptance of a subsequent offer except where the acceptance is contingent on the termination of the pre-existing purchase contract or lease. *(Amended 1/93)*

· **Standard of Practice 1-8**

REALTORS®, acting as agents or brokers of buyers/tenants, shall submit to buyers/tenants all offers and counter-offers until acceptance but have no obligation to continue to show properties to their clients after an offer has been accepted unless otherwise agreed in writing. REALTORS®, acting as agents or brokers of buyers/tenants, shall recommend that buyers/tenants obtain the advice of legal counsel if there is a question as to whether a pre-existing contract has been terminated. *(Adopted 1/93, Amended 1/99)*

· **Standard of Practice 1-9**

The obligation of REALTORS® to preserve confidential information (as defined by state law) provided by their clients in the course of any agency relationship or non-agency relationship recognized by law continues after termination of agency relationships or any non-agency relationships recognized by law. REALTORS® shall not knowingly, during or following the termination of professional relationships with their clients:

1) reveal confidential information of clients; or
2) use confidential information of clients to the disadvantage of clients; or
3) use confidential information of clients for the REALTOR®'s advantage or the advantage of third parties unless:
   a) clients consent after full disclosure; or
   b) REALTORS® are required by court order; or
   c) it is the intention of a client to commit a crime and the information is necessary to prevent the crime; or
   d) it is necessary to defend a REALTOR® or the REALTOR®'s employees or associates against an accusation of wrongful conduct.

Information concerning latent material defects is not considered confidential information under this Code of Ethics. *(Adopted 1/93, Amended 1/01)*

· **Standard of Practice 1-10**

REALTORS® shall, consistent with the terms and conditions of their real estate licensure and their property management agreement, competently manage the property of clients with due regard for the rights, safety and health of tenants and others lawfully on the premises. *(Adopted 1/95, Amended 1/00)*

· **Standard of Practice 1-11**

REALTORS® who are employed to maintain or manage a client's property shall exercise due diligence and make reasonable efforts to protect it against reasonably foreseeable contingencies and losses. *(Adopted 1/95)*

· **Standard of Practice 1-12**

When entering into listing contracts, REALTORS® must advise sellers/landlords of:

1) the REALTOR®'s company policies regarding cooperation and the amount(s) of any compensation that will be offered to subagents, buyer/tenant agents, and/or brokers acting in legally recognized non-agency capacities;

2) the fact that buyer/tenant agents or brokers, even if compensated by listing brokers, or by sellers/landlords may represent the interests of buyers/tenants; and
3) any potential for listing brokers to act as disclosed dual agents, e.g., buyer/tenant agents. *(Adopted 1/93, Renumbered 1/98, Amended 1/03)*

· **Standard of Practice 1-13**

When entering into buyer/tenant agreements, REALTORS® must advise potential clients of:

1) the REALTOR®'s company policies regarding cooperation;
2) the amount of compensation to be paid by the client;
3) the potential for additional or offsetting compensation from other brokers, from the seller or landlord, or from other parties;
4) any potential for the buyer/tenant representative to act as a disclosed dual agent, e.g., listing broker, subagent, landlord's agent, etc., and
5) the possibility that sellers or sellers' representatives may not treat the existence, terms, or conditions of offers as confidential unless confidentiality is required by law, regulation, or by any confidentiality agreement between the parties. *(Adopted 1/93, Renumbered 1/98, Amended 1/06)*

· **Standard of Practice 1-14**

Fees for preparing appraisals or other valuations shall not be contingent upon the amount of the appraisal or valuation. *(Adopted 1/02)*

· **Standard of Practice 1-15**

REALTORS®, in response to inquiries from buyers or cooperating brokers shall, with the sellers' approval, disclose the existence of offers on the property. Where disclosure is authorized, REALTORS® shall also disclose, if asked, whether offers were obtained by the listing licensee, another licensee in the listing firm, or by a cooperating broker. *(Adopted 1/03, Amended 1/09)*

· **Standard of Practice 1-16**

REALTORS® shall not access or use, or permit or enable others to access or use, listed or managed property on terms or conditions other than those authorized by the owner or seller. *(Adopted 1/12)*

Article 2

REALTORS® shall avoid exaggeration, misrepresentation, or concealment of pertinent facts relating to the property or the transaction. REALTORS® shall not, however, be obligated to discover latent defects in the property, to advise on matters outside the scope of their real estate license, or to disclose facts which are confidential under the scope of agency or non-agency relationships as defined by state law. *(Amended 1/00)*

· **Standard of Practice 2-1**

REALTORS® shall only be obligated to discover and disclose adverse factors reasonably apparent to someone with expertise in those areas required by their real estate licensing authority. Article 2 does not impose upon the REALTOR® the obligation of expertise in other professional or technical disciplines. *(Amended 1/96)*

· **Standard of Practice 2-2**

(Renumbered as Standard of Practice 1-12 1/98)

· **Standard of Practice 2-3**

(Renumbered as Standard of Practice 1-13 1/98)

· **Standard of Practice 2-4**

REALTORS® shall not be parties to the naming of a false consideration in any document, unless it be the naming of an obviously nominal consideration.

· **Standard of Practice 2-5**

Factors defined as "non-material" by law or regulation or which are expressly referenced in law or regulation as not being subject to disclosure are considered not "pertinent" for purposes of Article 2. *(Adopted 1/93)*

Article 3

REALTORS® shall cooperate with other brokers except when cooperation is not in the client's best interest. The obligation to cooperate does not include the obligation to share commissions, fees, or to otherwise compensate another broker. *(Amended 1/95)*

• **Standard of Practice 3-1**

REALTORS®, acting as exclusive agents or brokers of sellers/ landlords, establish the terms and conditions of offers to cooperate. Unless expressly indicated in offers to cooperate, cooperating brokers may not assume that the offer of cooperation includes an offer of compensation. Terms of compensation, if any, shall be ascertained by cooperating brokers before beginning efforts to accept the offer of cooperation. *(Amended 1/99)*

• **Standard of Practice 3-2**

Any change in compensation offered for cooperative services must be communicated to the other REALTOR® prior to the time that REALTOR® submits an offer to purchase/lease the property. After a REALTOR® has submitted an offer to purchase or lease property, the listing broker may not attempt to unilaterally modify the offered compensation with respect to that cooperative transaction. *(Amended 1/14)*

• **Standard of Practice 3-3**

Standard of Practice 3-2 does not preclude the listing broker and cooperating broker from entering into an agreement to change cooperative compensation. *(Adopted 1/94)*

• **Standard of Practice 3-4**

REALTORS®, acting as listing brokers, have an affirmative obligation to disclose the existence of dual or variable rate commission arrangements (i.e., listings where one amount of commission is payable if the listing broker's firm is the procuring cause of sale/lease and a different amount of commission is payable if the sale/lease results through the efforts of the seller/landlord or a cooperating broker). The listing broker shall, as soon as practical, disclose the existence of such arrangements to potential cooperating brokers and shall, in response to inquiries from cooperating brokers, disclose the differential that would result in a cooperative transaction or in a sale/lease that results through the efforts of the seller/landlord. If the cooperating broker is a buyer/tenant representative, the buyer/tenant representative must disclose such information to their client before the client makes an offer to purchase or lease. *(Amended 1/02)*

• **Standard of Practice 3-5**

It is the obligation of subagents to promptly disclose all pertinent facts to the principal's agent prior to as well as after a purchase or lease agreement is executed. *(Amended 1/93)*

• **Standard of Practice 3-6**

REALTORS® shall disclose the existence of accepted offers, including offers with unresolved contingencies, to any broker seeking cooperation. *(Adopted 5/86, Amended 1/04)*

• **Standard of Practice 3-7**

When seeking information from another REALTOR® concerning property under a management or listing agreement, REALTORS® shall disclose their REALTOR® status and whether their interest is personal or on behalf of a client and, if on behalf of a client, their relationship with the client. *(Amended 1/11)*

• **Standard of Practice 3-8**

REALTORS® shall not misrepresent the availability of access to show or inspect a listed property. *(Amended 11/87)*

• **Standard of Practice 3-9**

REALTORS® shall not provide access to listed property on terms other than those established by the owner or the listing broker. *(Adopted 1/10)*

• **Standard of Practice 3-10**

The duty to cooperate established in Article 3 relates to the obligation to share information on listed property, and to make property available to other brokers for showing to prospective purchasers/tenants when it is in the best interests of sellers/landlords. *(Adopted 1/11)*

Article 4

REALTORS® shall not acquire an interest in or buy or present offers from themselves, any member of their immediate families, their firms or any member thereof, or any entities in which they have any ownership interest, any real property without making their true position known to the owner or the owner's agent or broker. In selling property they own, or in which they have any interest, REALTORS® shall reveal their ownership or interest in writing to the purchaser or the purchaser's representative. *(Amended 1/00)*

• **Standard of Practice 4-1**

For the protection of all parties, the disclosures required by Article 4 shall be in writing and provided by REALTORS® prior to the signing of any contract. *(Adopted 2/86)*

Article 5

REALTORS® shall not undertake to provide professional services concerning a property or its value where they have a present or contemplated interest unless such interest is specifically disclosed to all affected parties.

Article 6

REALTORS® shall not accept any commission, rebate, or profit on expenditures made for their client, without the client's knowledge and consent.

When recommending real estate products or services (e.g., homeowner's insurance, warranty programs, mortgage financing, title insurance, etc.), REALTORS® shall disclose to the client or customer to whom the recommendation is made any financial benefits or fees, other than real estate referral fees, the REALTOR® or REALTOR®'s firm may receive as a direct result of such recommendation. *(Amended 1/99)*

• **Standard of Practice 6-1**

REALTORS® shall not recommend or suggest to a client or a customer the use of services of another organization or business entity in which they have a direct interest without disclosing such interest at the time of the recommendation or suggestion. *(Amended 5/88)*

Article 7

In a transaction, REALTORS® shall not accept compensation from more than one party, even if permitted by law, without disclosure to all parties and the informed consent of the REALTOR®'s client or clients. *(Amended 1/93)*

Article 8

REALTORS® shall keep in a special account in an appropriate financial institution, separated from their own funds, monies coming into their possession in trust for other persons, such as escrows, trust funds, clients' monies, and other like items.

Article 9

REALTORS®, for the protection of all parties, shall assure whenever possible that all agreements related to real estate transactions including, but not limited to, listing and representation agreements, purchase contracts, and leases are in writing in clear and understandable language expressing the specific terms, conditions, obligations and commitments of the parties. A copy of each agreement shall be furnished to each party to such agreements upon their signing or initialing. *(Amended 1/04)*

- **Standard of Practice 9-1**

    For the protection of all parties, REALTORS® shall use reasonable care to ensure that documents pertaining to the purchase, sale, or lease of real estate are kept current through the use of written extensions or amendments. *(Amended 1/93)*

- **Standard of Practice 9-2**

    When assisting or enabling a client or customer in establishing a contractual relationship (e.g., listing and representation agreements, purchase agreements, leases, etc.) electronically, REALTORS® shall make reasonable efforts to explain the nature and disclose the specific terms of the contractual relationship being established prior to it being agreed to by a contracting party. *(Adopted 1/07)*

Duties to the Public

Article 10

REALTORS® shall not deny equal professional services to any person for reasons of race, color, religion, sex, handicap, familial status, national origin, sexual orientation, or gender identity. REALTORS® shall not be parties to any plan or agreement to discriminate against a person or persons on the basis of race, color, religion, sex, handicap, familial status, national origin, sexual orientation, or gender identity. *(Amended 1/14)*

REALTORS®, in their real estate employment practices, shall not discriminate against any person or persons on the basis of race, color, religion, sex, handicap, familial status, national origin, sexual orientation, or gender identity. *(Amended 1/14)*

- **Standard of Practice 10-1**

    When involved in the sale or lease of a residence, REALTORS® shall not volunteer information regarding the racial, religious or ethnic composition of any neighborhood nor shall they engage in any activity which may result in panic selling, however, REALTORS® may provide other demographic information. *(Adopted 1/94, Amended 1/06)*

- **Standard of Practice 10-2**

    When not involved in the sale or lease of a residence, REALTORS® may provide demographic information related to a property, transaction or professional assignment to a party if such demographic information is (a) deemed by the REALTOR® to be needed to assist with or complete, in a manner consistent with Article 10, a real estate transaction or professional assignment and (b) is obtained or derived from a recognized, reliable, independent, and impartial source. The source of such information and any additions, deletions, modifications, interpretations, or other changes shall be disclosed in reasonable detail. *(Adopted 1/05, Renumbered 1/06)*

- **Standard of Practice 10-3**

    REALTORS® shall not print, display or circulate any statement or advertisement with respect to selling or renting of a property that indicates any preference, limitations or discrimination based on race, color, religion, sex, handicap, familial status, national origin, sexual orientation, or gender identity. *(Adopted 1/94, Renumbered 1/05 and 1/06, Amended 1/14)*

- **Standard of Practice 10-4**

    As used in Article 10 "real estate employment practices" relates to employees and independent contractors providing real estate-related services and the administrative and clerical staff directly supporting those individuals. *(Adopted 1/00, Renumbered 1/05 and 1/06)*

Article 11

The services which REALTORS® provide to their clients and customers shall conform to the standards of practice and competence which are reasonably expected in the specific real estate disciplines in which they engage; specifically, residential real estate brokerage, real property management, commercial and industrial real estate brokerage, land brokerage, real estate appraisal, real estate counseling, real estate syndication, real estate auction, and international real estate.

REALTORS® shall not undertake to provide specialized professional services concerning a type of property or service that is outside their field of competence unless they engage the assistance of one who is competent on such types of property or service, or unless the facts are fully disclosed to the client. Any persons engaged to provide such assistance shall be so identified to the client and their contribution to the assignment should be set forth. *(Amended 1/10)*

- **Standard of Practice 11-1**

    When REALTORS® prepare opinions of real property value or price they must:
    1) be knowledgeable about the type of property being valued,
    2) have access to the information and resources necessary to formulate an accurate opinion, and
    3) be familiar with the area where the subject property is located

    unless lack of any of these is disclosed to the party requesting the opinion in advance.

    When an opinion of value or price is prepared other than in pursuit of a listing or to assist a potential purchaser in formulating a purchase offer, the opinion shall include the following unless the party requesting the opinion requires a specific type of report or different data set:
    1) identification of the subject property
    2) date prepared
    3) defined value or price
    4) limiting conditions, including statements of purpose(s) and intended user(s)
    5) any present or contemplated interest, including the possibility of representing the seller/landlord or buyers/tenants
    6) basis for the opinion, including applicable market data
    7) if the opinion is not an appraisal, a statement to that effect
    8) disclosure of whether and when a physical inspection of the property's exterior was conducted
    9) disclosure of whether and when a physical inspection of the property's interior was conducted
    10) disclosure of whether the REALTOR® has any conflicts of interest *(Amended 1/14)*

- **Standard of Practice 11-2**

    The obligations of the Code of Ethics in respect of real estate disciplines other than appraisal shall be interpreted and applied in accordance with the standards of competence and practice which clients and the public reasonably require to protect their rights and interests considering the complexity of the transaction, the availability of expert assistance, and, where the REALTOR® is an agent or subagent, the obligations of a fiduciary. *(Adopted 1/95)*

- **Standard of Practice 11-3**

    When REALTORS® provide consultive services to clients which involve advice or counsel for a fee (not a commission), such advice shall be rendered in an objective manner and the fee shall not be contingent on the substance of the advice or counsel given. If brokerage or transaction services are to be provided in addition to consultive services, a separate compensation may be paid with prior agreement between the client and REALTOR®. *(Adopted 1/96)*

- **Standard of Practice 11-4**

    The competency required by Article 11 relates to services contracted for between REALTORS® and their clients or customers; the duties expressly *rules + keys*

Can send to Cards to everyone in Neighborhood NOT Specific to An address I want to list

imposed by the Code of Ethics; and the duties imposed by law or regulation. *(Adopted 1/02)*

Article 12

REALTORS® shall be honest and truthful in their real estate communications and shall present a true picture in their advertising, marketing, and other representations. REALTORS® shall ensure that their status as real estate professionals is readily apparent in their advertising, marketing, and other representations, and that the recipients of all real estate communications are, or have been, notified that those communications are from a real estate professional. *(Amended 1/08)*

- **Standard of Practice 12-1**

  REALTORS® may use the term "free" and similar terms in their advertising and in other representations provided that all terms governing availability of the offered product or service are clearly disclosed at the same time. *(Amended 1/97)*

- **Standard of Practice 12-2**

  REALTORS® may represent their services as "free" or without cost even if they expect to receive compensation from a source other than their client provided that the potential for the REALTOR® to obtain a benefit from a third party is clearly disclosed at the same time. *(Amended 1/97)*

- **Standard of Practice 12-3**

  The offering of premiums, prizes, merchandise discounts or other inducements to list, sell, purchase, or lease is not, in itself, unethical even if receipt of the benefit is contingent on listing, selling, purchasing, or leasing through the REALTOR® making the offer. However, REALTORS® must exercise care and candor in any such advertising or other public or private representations so that any party interested in receiving or otherwise benefiting from the REALTOR®'s offer will have clear, thorough, advance understanding of all the terms and conditions of the offer. The offering of any inducements to do business is subject to the limitations and restrictions of state law and the ethical obligations established by any applicable Standard of Practice. *(Amended 1/95)*

- **Standard of Practice 12-4**

  REALTORS® shall not offer for sale/lease or advertise property without authority. When acting as listing brokers or as subagents, REALTORS® shall not quote a price different from that agreed upon with the seller/landlord. *(Amended 1/93)*

- **Standard of Practice 12-5**

  REALTORS® shall not advertise nor permit any person employed by or affiliated with them to advertise real estate services or listed property in any medium (e.g., electronically, print, radio, television, etc.) without disclosing the name of that REALTOR®'s firm in a reasonable and readily apparent manner. This Standard of Practice acknowledges that disclosing the name of the firm may not be practical in electronic displays of limited information (e.g., "thumbnails", text messages, "tweets", etc.). Such displays are exempt from the disclosure requirement established in this Standard of Practice, but only when linked to a display that includes all required disclosures. *(Adopted 11/86, Amended 1/11)*

- **Standard of Practice 12-6**

  REALTORS®, when advertising unlisted real property for sale/lease in which they have an ownership interest, shall disclose their status as both owners/landlords and as REALTORS® or real estate licensees. *(Amended 1/93)*

- **Standard of Practice 12-7**

  Only REALTORS® who participated in the transaction as the listing broker or cooperating broker (selling broker) may claim to have "sold" the property.

Prior to closing, a cooperating broker may post a "sold" sign only with the consent of the listing broker. *(Amended 1/96)*

- **Standard of Practice 12-8**

  The obligation to present a true picture in representations to the public includes information presented, provided, or displayed on REALTORS®' websites. REALTORS® shall use reasonable efforts to ensure that information on their websites is current. When it becomes apparent that information on a REALTOR®'s website is no longer current or accurate, REALTORS® shall promptly take corrective action. *(Adopted 1/07)*

- **Standard of Practice 12-9**

  REALTOR® firm websites shall disclose the firm's name and state(s) of licensure in a reasonable and readily apparent manner.

  Websites of REALTORS® and non-member licensees affiliated with a REALTOR® firm shall disclose the firm's name and that REALTOR®'s or non-member licensee's state(s) of licensure in a reasonable and readily apparent manner. *(Adopted 1/07)*

- **Standard of Practice 12-10**

  REALTORS®' obligation to present a true picture in their advertising and representations to the public includes Internet content posted, and the URLs and domain names they use, and prohibits REALTORS® from:
  1) engaging in deceptive or unauthorized framing of real estate brokerage websites;
  2) manipulating (e.g., presenting content developed by others) listing and other content in any way that produces a deceptive or misleading result;
  3) deceptively using metatags, keywords or other devices/methods to direct, drive, or divert Internet traffic; or
  4) presenting content developed by others without either attribution or without permission, or
  5) to otherwise mislead consumers. *(Adopted 1/07, Amended 1/13)*

- **Standard of Practice 12-11**

  REALTORS® intending to share or sell consumer information gathered via the Internet shall disclose that possibility in a reasonable and readily apparent manner. *(Adopted 1/07)*

- **Standard of Practice 12-12**

  REALTORS® shall not:
  1) use URLs or domain names that present less than a true picture, or
  2) register URLs or domain names which, if used, would present less than a true picture. *(Adopted 1/08)*

- **Standard of Practice 12-13**

  The obligation to present a true picture in advertising, marketing, and representations allows REALTORS® to use and display only professional designations, certifications, and other credentials to which they are legitimately entitled. *(Adopted 1/08)*

Article 13

REALTORS® shall not engage in activities that constitute the unauthorized practice of law and shall recommend that legal counsel be obtained when the interest of any party to the transaction requires it.

Article 14

If charged with unethical practice or asked to present evidence or to cooperate in any other way, in any professional standards proceeding or investigation, REALTORS® shall place all pertinent facts before the proper tribunals of the Member Board or affiliated institute, society, or council in which membership is held and shall take no action to disrupt or obstruct such processes. *(Amended 1/99)*

- **Standard of Practice 14-1**

REALTORS® shall not be subject to disciplinary proceedings in more than one Board of REALTORS® or affiliated institute, society, or council in which they hold membership with respect to alleged violations of the Code of Ethics relating to the same transaction or event. *(Amended 1/95)*

- **Standard of Practice 14-2**

REALTORS® shall not make any unauthorized disclosure or dissemination of the allegations, findings, or decision developed in connection with an ethics hearing or appeal or in connection with an arbitration hearing or procedural review. *(Amended 1/92)*

- **Standard of Practice 14-3**

REALTORS® shall not obstruct the Board's investigative or professional standards proceedings by instituting or threatening to institute actions for libel, slander, or defamation against any party to a professional standards proceeding or their witnesses based on the filing of an arbitration request, an ethics complaint, or testimony given before any tribunal. *(Adopted 11/87, Amended 1/99)*

- **Standard of Practice 14-4**

REALTORS® shall not intentionally impede the Board's investigative or disciplinary proceedings by filing multiple ethics complaints based on the same event or transaction. *(Adopted 11/88)*

Duties to REALTORS®

Article 15

REALTORS® shall not knowingly or recklessly make false or misleading statements about other real estate professionals, their businesses, or their business practices. *(Amended 1/12)*

- **Standard of Practice 15-1**

REALTORS® shall not knowingly or recklessly file false or unfounded ethics complaints. *(Adopted 1/00)*

- **Standard of Practice 15-2**

The obligation to refrain from making false or misleading statements about other real estate professionals, their businesses, and their business practices includes the duty to not knowingly or recklessly publish, repeat, retransmit, or republish false or misleading statements made by others. This duty applies whether false or misleading statements are repeated in person, in writing, by technological means (e.g., the Internet), or by any other means. *(Adopted 1/07, Amended 1/12)*

- **Standard of Practice 15-3**

The obligation to refrain from making false or misleading statements about other real estate professionals, their businesses, and their business practices includes the duty to publish a clarification about or to remove statements made by others on electronic media the REALTOR® controls once the REALTOR® knows the statement is false or misleading. *(Adopted 1/10, Amended 1/12)*

Article 16

REALTORS® shall not engage in any practice or take any action inconsistent with exclusive representation or exclusive brokerage relationship agreements that other REALTORS® have with clients. *(Amended 1/04)*

- **Standard of Practice 16-1**

Article 16 is not intended to prohibit aggressive or innovative business practices which are otherwise ethical and does not prohibit disagreements with other REALTORS® involving commission, fees,

compensation or other forms of payment or expenses. *(Adopted 1/93, Amended 1/95)*

- **Standard of Practice 16-2**

Article 16 does not preclude REALTORS® from making general announcements to prospects describing their services and the terms of their availability even though some recipients may have entered into agency agreements or other exclusive relationships with another REALTOR®. A general telephone canvass, general mailing or distribution addressed to all prospects in a given geographical area or in a given profession, business, club, or organization, or other classification or group is deemed "general" for purposes of this standard. *(Amended 1/04)*

Article 16 is intended to recognize as unethical two basic types of solicitations:

First, telephone or personal solicitations of property owners who have been identified by a real estate sign, multiple listing compilation, or other information service as having exclusively listed their property with another REALTOR® and

Second, mail or other forms of written solicitations of prospects whose properties are exclusively listed with another REALTOR® when such solicitations are not part of a general mailing but are directed specifically to property owners identified through compilations of current listings, "for sale" or "for rent" signs, or other sources of information required by Article 3 and Multiple Listing Service rules to be made available to other REALTORS® under offers of subagency or cooperation. *(Amended 1/04)*

- **Standard of Practice 16-3**

Article 16 does not preclude REALTORS® from contacting the client of another broker for the purpose of offering to provide, or entering into a contract to provide, a different type of real estate service unrelated to the type of service currently being provided (e.g., property management as opposed to brokerage) or from offering the same type of service for property not subject to other brokers' exclusive agreements. However, information received through a Multiple Listing Service or any other offer of cooperation may not be used to target clients of other REALTORS® to whom such offers to provide services may be made. *(Amended 1/04)*

- **Standard of Practice 16-4**

REALTORS® shall not solicit a listing which is currently listed exclusively with another broker. However, if the listing broker, when asked by the REALTOR®, refuses to disclose the expiration date and nature of such listing, i.e., an exclusive right to sell, an exclusive agency, open listing, or other form of contractual agreement between the listing broker and the client, the REALTOR® may contact the owner to secure such information and may discuss the terms upon which the REALTOR® might take a future listing or, alternatively, may take a listing to become effective upon expiration of any existing exclusive listing. *(Amended 1/94)*

- **Standard of Practice 16-5**

REALTORS® shall not solicit buyer/tenant agreements from buyers/tenants who are subject to exclusive buyer/tenant agreements. However, if asked by a REALTOR®, the broker refuses to disclose the expiration date of the exclusive buyer/tenant agreement, the REALTOR® may contact the buyer/tenant to secure such information and may discuss the terms upon which the REALTOR® might enter into a future buyer/tenant agreement or, alternatively, may enter into a buyer/tenant agreement to become effective upon the expiration of any existing exclusive buyer/tenant agreement. *(Adopted 1/94, Amended 1/98)*

If you don't have anything good to say don't say it

- **Standard of Practice 16-6**

  When REALTORS® are contacted by the client of another REALTOR® regarding the creation of an exclusive relationship to provide the same type of service, and REALTORS® have not directly or indirectly initiated such discussions, they may discuss the terms upon which they might enter into a future agreement or, alternatively, may enter into an agreement which becomes effective upon expiration of any existing exclusive agreement. *(Amended 1/98)*

- **Standard of Practice 16-7**

  The fact that a prospect has retained a REALTOR® as an exclusive representative or exclusive broker in one or more past transactions does not preclude other REALTORS® from seeking such prospect's future business. *(Amended 1/04)*

- **Standard of Practice 16-8**

  The fact that an exclusive agreement has been entered into with a REALTOR® shall not preclude or inhibit any other REALTOR® from entering into a similar agreement after the expiration of the prior agreement. *(Amended 1/98)*

- **Standard of Practice 16-9**

  REALTORS®, prior to entering into a representation agreement, have an affirmative obligation to make reasonable efforts to determine whether the prospect is subject to a current, valid exclusive agreement to provide the same type of real estate service. *(Amended 1/04)*

- **Standard of Practice 16-10**

  REALTORS®, acting as buyer or tenant representatives or brokers, shall disclose that relationship to the seller/landlord's representative or broker at first contact and shall provide written confirmation of that disclosure to the seller/landlord's representative or broker not later than execution of a purchase agreement or lease. *(Amended 1/04)*

- **Standard of Practice 16-11**

  On unlisted property, REALTORS® acting as buyer/tenant representatives or brokers shall disclose that relationship to the seller/landlord at first contact for that buyer/tenant and shall provide written confirmation of such disclosure to the seller/landlord not later than execution of any purchase or lease agreement. *(Amended 1/04)*

  REALTORS® shall make any request for anticipated compensation from the seller/landlord at first contact. *(Amended 1/98)*

- **Standard of Practice 16-12**

  REALTORS®, acting as representatives or brokers of sellers/landlords or as subagents of listing brokers, shall disclose that relationship to buyers/tenants as soon as practicable and shall provide written confirmation of such disclosure to buyers/tenants not later than execution of any purchase or lease agreement. *(Amended 1/04)*

- **Standard of Practice 16-13**

  All dealings concerning property exclusively listed, or with buyer/tenants who are subject to an exclusive agreement shall be carried on with the client's representative or broker, and not with the client, except with the consent of the client's representative or broker or except where such dealings are initiated by the client.

  Before providing substantive services (such as writing a purchase offer or presenting a CMA) to prospects, REALTORS® shall ask prospects whether they are a party to any exclusive representation agreement. REALTORS® shall not knowingly provide substantive services concerning a prospective transaction to prospects who are parties to exclusive representation agreements, except with the consent of the prospects' exclusive representatives or at the direction of prospects. *(Adopted 1/93, Amended 1/04)*

- **Standard of Practice 16-14**

  REALTORS® are free to enter into contractual relationships or to negotiate with sellers/landlords, buyers/tenants or others who are not subject to an exclusive agreement but shall not knowingly obligate them to pay more than one commission except with their informed consent. *(Amended 1/98)*

- **Standard of Practice 16-15**

  In cooperative transactions REALTORS® shall compensate cooperating REALTORS® (principal brokers) and shall not compensate nor offer to compensate, directly or indirectly, any of the sales licensees employed by or affiliated with other REALTORS® without the prior express knowledge and consent of the cooperating broker.

- **Standard of Practice 16-16**

  REALTORS®, acting as subagents or buyer/tenant representatives or brokers, shall not use the terms of an offer to purchase/lease to attempt to modify the listing broker's offer of compensation to subagents or buyer/tenant representatives or brokers nor make the submission of an executed offer to purchase/lease contingent on the listing broker's agreement to modify the offer of compensation. *(Amended 1/04)*

- **Standard of Practice 16-17**

  REALTORS®, acting as subagents or as buyer/tenant representatives or brokers, shall not attempt to extend a listing broker's offer of cooperation and/or compensation to other brokers without the consent of the listing broker. *(Amended 1/04)*

- **Standard of Practice 16-18**

  REALTORS® shall not use information obtained from listing brokers through offers to cooperate made through multiple listing services or through other offers of cooperation to refer listing brokers' clients to other brokers or to create buyer/tenant relationships with listing brokers' clients, unless such use is authorized by listing brokers. *(Amended 1/02)*

- **Standard of Practice 16-19**

  Signs giving notice of property for sale, rent, lease, or exchange shall not be placed on property without consent of the seller/landlord. *(Amended 1/93)*

- **Standard of Practice 16-20**

  REALTORS®, prior to or after their relationship with their current firm is terminated, shall not induce clients of their current firm to cancel exclusive contractual agreements between the client and that firm. This does not preclude REALTORS® (principals) from establishing agreements with their associated licensees governing assignability of exclusive agreements. *(Adopted 1/98, Amended 1/10)*

Article 17

In the event of contractual disputes or specific non-contractual disputes as defined in Standard of Practice 17-4 between REALTORS® (principals) associated with different firms, arising out of their relationship as REALTORS®, the REALTORS® shall mediate the dispute if the Board requires its members to mediate. If the dispute is not resolved through mediation, or if mediation is not required, REALTORS® shall submit the dispute to arbitration in accordance with the policies of the Board rather than litigate the matter.

In the event clients of REALTORS® wish to mediate or arbitrate contractual disputes arising out of real estate transactions, REALTORS® shall mediate or arbitrate those disputes in accordance with the policies of the Board, provided the clients agree to be bound by any resulting agreement or award.

The obligation to participate in mediation and arbitration contemplated by this Article includes the obligation of REALTORS® (principals) to cause their firms to mediate and arbitrate and be bound by any resulting agreement or award. *(Amended 1/12)*

- **Standard of Practice 17-1**

The filing of litigation and refusal to withdraw from it by REALTORS® in an arbitrable matter constitutes a refusal to arbitrate. *(Adopted 2/86)*

- **Standard of Practice 17-2**

Article 17 does not require REALTORS® to mediate in those circumstances when all parties to the dispute advise the Board in writing that they choose not to mediate through the Board's facilities. The fact that all parties decline to participate in mediation does not relieve REALTORS® of the duty to arbitrate.

Article 17 does not require REALTORS® to arbitrate in those circumstances when all parties to the dispute advise the Board in writing that they choose not to arbitrate before the Board. *(Amended 1/12)*

- **Standard of Practice 17-3**

REALTORS®, when acting solely as principals in a real estate transaction, are not obligated to arbitrate disputes with other REALTORS® absent a specific written agreement to the contrary. *(Adopted 1/96)*

- **Standard of Practice 17-4**

Specific non-contractual disputes that are subject to arbitration pursuant to Article 17 are:

1) Where a listing broker has compensated a cooperating broker and another cooperating broker subsequently claims to be the procuring cause of the sale or lease. In such cases the complainant may name the first cooperating broker as respondent and arbitration may proceed without the listing broker being named as a respondent. When arbitration occurs between two (or more) cooperating brokers and where the listing broker is not a party, the amount in dispute and the amount of any potential resulting award is limited to the amount paid to the respondent by the listing broker and any amount credited or paid to a party to the transaction at the direction of the respondent. Alternatively, if the complaint is brought against the listing broker, the listing broker may name the first cooperating broker as a third-party respondent. In either instance the decision of the hearing panel as to procuring cause shall be conclusive with respect to all current or subsequent claims of the parties for compensation arising out of the underlying cooperative transaction. *(Adopted 1/97, Amended 1/07)*

2) Where a buyer or tenant representative is compensated by the seller or landlord, and not by the listing broker, and the listing broker, as a result, reduces the commission owed by the seller or landlord and, subsequent to such actions, another cooperating broker claims to be the procuring cause of sale or lease. In such cases the complainant may name the first cooperating broker as respondent and arbitration may proceed without the listing broker being named as a respondent. When arbitration occurs between two (or more) cooperating brokers and where the listing broker is not a party, the amount in dispute and the amount of any potential resulting award is limited to the amount paid to the respondent by the seller or landlord and any amount credited or paid to a party to the transaction at the direction of the respondent. Alternatively, if the complaint is brought against the listing broker, the listing broker may name the first cooperating broker as a third-party respondent. In either instance the decision of the hearing panel as to procuring cause shall be conclusive with respect to all current or subsequent claims of the parties for compensation arising out of the underlying cooperative transaction. *(Adopted 1/97, Amended 1/07)*

3) Where a buyer or tenant representative is compensated by the buyer or tenant and, as a result, the listing broker reduces the commission owed by the seller or landlord and, subsequent to such actions, another cooperating broker claims to be the procuring cause of sale or lease. In such cases the complainant may name the first cooperating broker as respondent and arbitration may proceed without the listing broker being named as a respondent. Alternatively, if the complaint is brought against the listing broker, the listing broker may name the first cooperating broker as a third-party respondent. In either instance the decision of the hearing panel as to procuring cause shall be conclusive with respect to all current or subsequent claims of the parties for compensation arising out of the underlying cooperative transaction. *(Adopted 1/97)*

4) Where two or more listing brokers claim entitlement to compensation pursuant to open listings with a seller or landlord who agrees to participate in arbitration (or who requests arbitration) and who agrees to be bound by the decision. In cases where one of the listing brokers has been compensated by the seller or landlord, the other listing broker, as complainant, may name the first listing broker as respondent and arbitration may proceed between the brokers. *(Adopted 1/97)*

5) Where a buyer or tenant representative is compensated by the seller or landlord, and not by the listing broker, and the listing broker, as a result, reduces the commission owed by the seller or landlord and, subsequent to such actions, claims to be the procuring cause of sale or lease. In such cases arbitration shall be between the listing broker and the buyer or tenant representative and the amount in dispute is limited to the amount of the reduction of commission to which the listing broker agreed. *(Adopted 1/05)*

- **Standard of Practice 17-5**

The obligation to arbitrate established in Article 17 includes disputes between REALTORS® (principals) in different states in instances where, absent an established inter-association arbitration agreement, the REALTOR® (principal) requesting arbitration agrees to submit to the jurisdiction of, travel to, participate in, and be bound by any resulting award rendered in arbitration conducted by the respondent(s) REALTOR®'s association, in instances where the respondent(s) REALTOR®'s association determines that an arbitrable issue exists. *(Adopted 1/07)*

Explanatory Notes

The reader should be aware of the following policies which have been approved by the Board of Directors of the National Association:

In filing a charge of an alleged violation of the Code of Ethics by a REALTOR®, the charge must read as an alleged violation of one or more Articles of the Code. Standards of Practice may be cited in support of the charge.

The Standards of Practice serve to clarify the ethical obligations imposed by the various Articles and supplement, and do not substitute for, the Case Interpretations in *Interpretations of the Code of Ethics.*

Modifications to existing Standards of Practice and additional new Standards of Practice are approved from time to time. Readers are cautioned to ensure that the most recent publications are utilized.

166-288-14 (01/14 VG)

For information about the Code's centennial go to: *www.realtor.org/coe100*

430 North Michigan Avenue • Chicago, IL 60611-4087
800.874.6500 • www.REALTOR.org

Chapter 1: True/False Questions

Learning Objective #1
1. **True.** The excuse of "protecting my client's best interests" is no excuse for breaking the law.
2. **False.** Some philosophy professors say that ethics and morality are synonymous; others do not agree.

Learning Objective #2
1. **False.** A written code has little meaning without open discussion on the tenets of the code for business practice.
2. **False.** Including ethics in the business school curriculum is required by the accreditation standards of the Association to Advance Collegiate Schools of Business (AACSB).

Learning Objective #3
1. **True.** It is difficult for schools to incorporate courses on technology, globalization, environmental issues, and ethics into a given framework of semester hours already crowded with other required courses.
2. **False.** Internet research has been a boon to students when used properly; unfortunately, it is also used for unethical plagiarizing as would be the case for Maria.

Chapter 1: Review Questions

1. **c.** The concept of situational ethics allows for making changes to what is considered the right thing to do depending on the circumstances of the particular situation.
2. **c.** Bad publicity eventually is forgotten. The loss of one's life savings can never be recovered.
3. **c.** In many cases, ethics go beyond the limitations of laws.
4. **c.** The investigation was focused on the setting up of tax shelters to assist clients with evading taxes.
5. **c.** The problem occurred when the accounting firm gave advice to a major client that led to tax evasion and fraud.
6. **b.** It has been found that the act of sitting down to discuss and formulate a Code of Ethics can be even more important than the actual results.
7. **c.** Values and Conscience are reflected downward from the one at the top of the organization.
8. **c.** The rules and regulations for the use of an MLS or the proper procedures for lockboxes are usually set by the local association or MLS system.
9. **c.** Agents who are willing to spend time with low-income renters are often "heroes" to the consumers.
10. **a.** The Better Business Bureau was the first to officially promote fairness and integrity in the market place.
11. **d.** The calculation of grade point averages is done mathematically and should not be subject to unethical behavior.
12. **c.** The news coverage of multiple corporate scandals emphasized the need for more study of business ethics.

13. **c.** Directly copying material from the internet has become a major issue of cheating in schools today.
14. **c.** The use of steroids and other performance-enhancing drugs is what has drawn the most attention from the media covering the sports world.
15. **d.** The war room was not covered in this chapter on ethical behavior.

Chapter 2: True/False Questions

Learning Objective #1

1. **False.** Ethical behavior on the part of real estate professionals is important for all aspects of their work, not just because of the financial investment of their clients.
2. **False.** ARELLO promotes uniform standards for state licensing laws and provides guidelines for pre- and post-licensing courses.

Learning Objective #2

1. **True.** Unfortunately, most buyers and even some sellers did believe that the agent working with the buyers did represent the buyer, but in fact the fiduciary duty was to the seller.
2. **False.** Megan's Law is the name given to the law that requires every jurisdiction to make available the names of released sex offenders to the community. There is no requirement for a licensee to make such disclosure.

Learning Objective #3

1. **False.** Depending on state law, real estate settlements may be done by attorneys, title and escrow agents, or in escrow (Western states).
2. **True.** Forcing a borrower into a lower status loan due to his nationality is not only predatory but is also a fair housing violation.

Chapter 2: Case Studies

Case Study #1—Multiple Clients

1. **c.** George walked into Martin's office after seeing the For Sale sign on the property.
2. **d.** The XYZ broker has a brokerage relationship with all three clients and must take care to maintain confidentiality.

Case Study #2—For Sale by Owner (FSBO)

1. **d.** Marcia's pledge is to protect and promote the best interests of her client.
2. **d.** On first contact with the Gonzalezes, Marcia could discuss optional ways to include a buyer agent's commission in the sales price; if they refuse, she still owes it to her buyer client to show the property and proceed with a contract if so desired.

Case Study #3—Selling Your Own Listing

1. **b.** To avoid any chance of conflict of interest, Tony should have discussed bringing in another agent to represent the Lees.
2. **d.** The inherent hazard of dual agency is that neither client feels fairly represented.

Case Study #4—Megan's Law

1. **c.** Gloria should have discussed the need for possible disclosure. If the Martinezes refused, she might not want to take the listing.
2. **a.** Purchasers who want to be fully represented should contract with a buyer agent who will help them find whatever information they want.

Chapter 2: Review Questions

1. **d.** Real estate practitioners come from many different types of backgrounds.
2. **a.** The Association of Real Estate License Law Officials (ARELLO) promotes uniform standards for administering and enforcing state license law.
3. **b.** For most people, the purchase of a personal residence is the largest financial investment made.
4. **b.** Even though full fiduciary responsibility was due to the seller, the purchaser (customer) was to be treated honestly at all times.
5. **d.** Buyer agency became a hot news item in the late 1980's in California and soon spread across the country.
6. **b.** With designated agency, one agent from a company may represent the seller and another agent from the same company may represent the buyer. The broker remains in the position of a dual agent with responsibility to both clients.
7. **d.** With dual agency, the agent actually has two clients—both the buyer and the seller.
8. **b.** Having multiple clients can present a possible conflict of interest if they are all interested in purchasing the same property.
9. **d.** There are many aspects of a commercial transaction that can cause problems, but membership in multiple professional organizations would not be one of them.
10. **d.** In order to avoid any violation of the fair housing law, rejection of possible tenants should be based only on lack of financial qualification.
11. **d.** Jack will be subject to both the Code of Ethics that is part of the Uniform Standards of Professional Appraisal Practice (USPAP) and the NAR Code of Ethics.
12. **d.** It is never appropriate for a home inspector to encourage buyers to try to renegotiate the sales price based on the findings of the home inspection.
13. **d.** Depending on state law and local custom, closings may be done by attorneys, title and escrow agents, or in escrow.
14. **d.** A value check or opinion of value may be prepared by a real estate broker, but it is not an appraisal and could not be used as the basis for a mortgage loan through Fannie Mae or other loan providers.
15. **d.** Differences in language, customs, and monetary system are all important factors, but the biggest challenge is probably that of differences in interpretation of what is ethical behavior.

Chapter 3: True/False Questions

Learning Objective #1
1. **False.** The 2½ hour orientation course fulfills the quadrennial requirement for taking a 2½ hour ethics course.
2. **False.** The sending of large electronic file attachments would most likely create a problem for a fellow REALTOR® and is included in the *Pathways to Professionalism* under Showing Respect for Peers.

Learning Objective #2
1. **False.** The laws regarding the disclosure of stigmatizing information, such as a murder, suicide, or other committed felony in a home, varies from state to state.
2. **False.** Any change to the offer of compensation to a cooperating broker must be made prior to an offer being made.

Learning Objective #3

1. **False.** Restricting his hiring to those of Hispanic origin would be a violation of fair housing law and to the NAR Code of Ethics, Article 10.

2. **False.** Although many agents still believe that only the listing agent can advertise the property as "sold," Article 12, SOP 12-7 is very clear that both the listing and the selling broker can advertise "sold" properties.

Learning Objective #4

1. **True.** Jane would be in violation of Article 16 if she initiated the call to Jack. Article 16, SOP 16-4 prohibits solicitation of a listing that is currently listed with another broker.

2. **False.** Mediation is a great way for two parties to reach an acceptable resolution for both parties. It does not sound like Broker Tom is interested in anything except receiving the total commission and he would probably opt to go for arbitration.

Chapter 3: Case Study

Case Study #1—Solving Your Own Problem

1. **d.** Agreeing to mediation would have taken place prior to the arbitration hearing. All of the other actions will be considered, but no one factor is the determining factor.

2. **c.** The role of the mediator is strictly to provide a comfortable atmosphere for the two parties to resolve their own difference. The mediator makes no final decision.

Chapter 3: Review Questions

1. **c.** The Code of Ethics was written in 1913 and became mandatory for membership in 1924.

2. **c.** As of 2000, all members of NAR must take 2½ hours of ethics training quadrennially.

3. **b.** The Greater Baltimore Board of REALTORS® was the first to incorporate a Code of Ethics into their Bylaws.

4. **b.** A "living document" is one that is carefully reviewed and edited on a regular basis.

5. **c.** The *Pathways to Professionalism* are recommended business practices, not part of the Code of Ethics.

6. **a.** Article 1 covers responsibility to clients and customers.

7. **c.** The Code of Ethics requires that other people's monies be kept in a separate account. State regulations specify the details of setting up and using such escrow accounts.

8. **d.** Article 9 specifies that all contracts, addenda, amendments, etcetera, must be in writing with a copy given to all parties; copies submitted electronically are accepted in most states today.

9. **c.** Profession is not one of the protected classes covered in Article 10: race, religion, color, national origin, sex, familial status, handicap, sexual orientation, and gender identity.

10. **d.** The three new areas of required disclosure do not include any disclose of stigmatizing factors.

11. **b.** The name of the firm is not required on electronic displays of limited information such as in a tweet.

12. **d.** Article 15 prohibits REALTORS® from making any false or misleading statements about other real estate professionals. It is best to avoid making any personal comments about fellow peers.

13. **c.** The disclosure of latent defects is covered in Article 2.

14. **d.** All of these may be taken into consideration, but the final determination for procuring cause is who initiated an uninterrupted series of events leading to a successful transaction.
15. **c.** An attempt at mediation would have been taken prior to an arbitration hearing.

Chapter 4: True/False Questions

Learning Objective #1
1.　**False.** Recommendations for sanctions are given in the NAR Code of Ethics and Arbitration Manual, but no specific sanction is designated for any individual violation.
2.　**False.** The decision of an ethics hearing panel can be appealed to the Board of Directors for procedural error. The decision of an arbitration hearing panel cannot be appealed.

Learning Objective #2
1.　**True.** Article 3, SOP 3-6 requires disclosure of all accepted offers, including those with unresolved contingencies. Article 1, SOP 1-15, also addresses the issue of disclosing the existence of offers on a property.
2.　**False.** Article 1, SOP 1-9, deals with the obligation of a REALTOR® to preserve confidential information even after the termination of the brokerage relationship. It clearly states that information concerning latent material defects is not considered confidential information.

Learning Objective #3
1.　**True.** Article 16 is focused on how REALTORS® interact with fellow REALTORS® with regard to the representation of their clients. There are often overlaps between Article 16 and the tenets of Articles 1 and 2 as they relate to the REALTORS® obligations to their clients.
2.　**False.** If the REALTOR® is not satisfied with the results of an arbitration panel hearing, they still have the right to resort to litigation.

Chapter 4: Review Questions

1. **b.** The parties involved in an ethics hearing have the right to have legal counsel present, but they may not send legal counsel to represent them at the hearing.
2. **b.** Similar to a grand jury, the Grievance Committee's sole purpose is to determine if there may have been a violation of one of the Articles of the Code of Ethics.
3. **c.** A REALTOR® hearing panel does not have the authority to impose monetary damages to the complainant but may impose a monetary penalty on the one making the violation.
4. **d.** Expulsion can only be from one to three years with reinstatement only by application.
5. **b.** For a first offense, the panel would be more interested in education than punishment. A suspension from membership must be for no less than 30 days or no more than one year.
6. **b.** A REALTOR® or member of the general public can file a complaint for a violation of one or more articles of the Code of Ethics. Complaints are not filed for specific Standards of Practice.
7. **c.** Article 3 specifically required REALTORS® to disclose the presence of existing offers.
8. **c.** Hearsay is not good enough; REALTOR® M should say she does not know what is planned.

9.   **b.** A violation of Article 2 often hinges on what is determined to be a pertinent fact related to the transaction.

10.   **a.** Article 3 requires disclosure of all accepted offers, whether they remain contingent or not.

11.   **a.** If the grievance committee decides that there may be a violation, the case will be forwarded to the Professional Standards committee for a panel hearing.

12.   **d.** Article 12 has undergone numerous changes in recent years; most recently, this has been dealing with the use of URLs and domain names.

13.   **c.** All contact should be made through the listing agent.

14.   **c.** If the client of a REALTOR® makes the initial contact with another REALTOR®, there is most likely no violation of Article 16.

15.   **a.** No one can prevent someone else from filing a legal suit. However, refusing to submit to arbitration in lieu of litigation is a violation of Article 17.

Chapter 5: True/False Questions

Learning Objective #1

1.   **True.** In general, retaining a listing within his own company would be a possible violation of Article 3, but if the sellers have given this instruction, there would be no violation.

2.   **False.** Whenever there are multiple offers, it is imperative that one be named primary before countering with others named as backups in numerical order.

Learning Objective #2

1.   **False.** There is a trend toward the formation of mega-firms, but there is also a trend toward the forming of small boutique, or niche market, companies.

2.   **False.** Limited service just means that the agent will not perform all of the normally expected duties of an agent. Fee-for-service assigns a numerical value for each service offered.

Learning Objective #3

1.   **False.** The National Do Not Call Registry applies to all calls made both within and outside the state.

2.   **False.** Appraisers also fall under the authority of the RESPA regulations.

Chapter 5: Case Studies

Case Study #1—Shopping the Contract

1.   **d.** Establishing a set time for presentation of all contracts is fine as long as this is the express wish of the seller—not the agent.

2.   **d.** No seller is obligated to accept any contract. The MLS listing is only information.

Case Study #2—ESL Clients

1.   **a.** The Nguyens were not Sally's clients; the loan officer and settlement agent are not REALTORS® so are not subject to the NAR Code. A case could be made based on Article 9, requiring everything to be in writing.

2.   **c.** Speaking the language does not help if there is no knowledge of American real estate law and practices.

Chapter 5: Review Questions

1. **c.** Magazine advertising is usually less in a hot market because properties sell more quickly.
2. **a.** Keeping a listing in the broker's "pocket" means it is not submitted to the local MLS.
3. **b.** An escalation clause must be carefully written so that there is an ultimate price that can be reached.
4. **c.** Only one offer can be made the primary contract; any others must be designated as back-ups.
5. **b.** It can be argued that delaying the presentation opens the opportunity for better offers to be received.
6. **a.** The Sherman Antitrust Act prohibits any action that may be considered a restraint of trade.
7. **b.** When all members of the team count their production to one person, it may be unfair to other agents.
8. **c.** The biggest problem with limited service representation is the possible confusion of who is responsible for which duties.
9. **c.** A broker can only offer a discount to the broker's own clients, never to someone else's client.
10. **c.** In today's virtual office, there is limited office space and no front desk requiring floor duty.
11. **c.** Under the Do-Not-Call Registry regulations, only clients with whom there has been a relationship with in the past 18 months may be called.
12. **c.** FACTA requires the destruction of all personal information about clients and customers.
13. **b.** The CAN-SPAM Act is an attempt to limit unsolicited e-mail messages.
14. **b.** No one is allowed to defray costs an agent would otherwise incur, such as the cost of a required continuing education course.
15. **c.** The SAFE Act falls under the Consumer Financial Protection Bureau and was created to protect the best interests of the consumer when obtaining a mortgage loan.

Chapter 6: True/False Questions

Learning Objective #1
1. **False.** Observance of the Golden Rule is a good start but can never guarantee correct ethical behavior.
2. **False.** No amount of study can ensure that you will always make the right ethical decision but a solid background will certainly provide a good source of help.

Learning Objective #2
1. **False.** In many cases, the ethical dilemma is a case of right versus right.
2. **False.** Of course, following the rules and regulations is necessary, but there are times when an ethical decision goes beyond the black-and-white status of the law.

Learning Objective #3
1. **False.** The ends-based principle is based on utilitarianism. The rule-based principle is based on the teachings of Immanuel Kant.
2. **True.** Moral courage takes hard work to develop. Kidder's seven checkpoints can be helpful.

Chapter 6: Review Questions

1. **d.** Conflict of Interest is not one of Tom Morris's "Six Tests for Ethical Action."
2. **a.** The publicity test is a good indicator of whether you would be ashamed or embarrassed by your decision.
3. **a.** Jonathan has proven to be a wise and good man and someone that she can look to for an example of ethical behavior.
4. **b.** One of the hazards of dual agency is that one of the parties may decide you are acting in the best interests of the other side, instead of providing equal representation.
5. **d.** With even a possible perceived conflict of interest, the decision making should be turned over to someone else.
6. **c.** Kidder's concept of paradigms is based on the ethical case of right versus right, never wrong.
7. **a.** Gloria is torn between the truth of the situation and loyalty to her client.
8. **b.** What is good for the individual in the short-term is often not the best for the community in the long-term.
9. **c.** Bringing in a top producer may help production in the short-term, but the detrimental effects to morale for the rest of the office could be disastrous in the long-term.
10. **d.** Brokers are often faced with a decision about letting go a well-loved, long-term veteran of an office. Justice without mercy can be tough.
11. **a.** This exemplifies the ends-based principle of decision making. The broker believes that his decision will provide the greatest good for the greatest number of people.
12. **c.** Care-based decisions take more into account than simple rules; the people are most important.
13. **c.** Decisions made on the rule-based principle leave no room for personal circumstances or compromise.
14. **c.** Both the Justice versus Mercy paradigm and care-based principle of decision making put the best interests of the person over the strict rules and regulations of the office.
15. **b.** Rushworth Kidder's book *Moral Courage* lists the seven checkpoints for developing a higher level of moral courage.

Note: Terms are defined as used in a real estate context.

actual conflict of interest the person responsible for making an ethical decision is directly affected by the outcome of the decision

adverse material defects defects in a property that directly affect normal operation

affiliated business arrangements ownership by real estate brokerage firm of other related real estate service providers (e.g., a mortgage company or a title company)

agency representation of the best interests of another party by an agent

agent licensee (including brokers and sales associates) acting in an agency relationship as defined by state law or regulation

American Association of Mortgage Brokers (AAMB) professional organization for mortgage brokers

Appraisal Institute professional organization for real estate appraisers

arbitration settlement of disputes, generally financial, between parties

arbitration hearing panel convenes to determine procuring cause and resolution of dispute

Association of Real Estate License Law Officials (ARELLO) promotes uniform standards for administering and enforcing state license laws

Association to Advance Collegiate Schools of Business (AACSB) accredits business schools

backup contract contract accepted to become prime if primary contract is terminated

Big Four the four largest accounting/auditing firms in the United States

buyer agency a contractual relationship between a broker and a purchaser client

buyer agent agent who has a brokerage relationship with purchaser client

care-based principle making a decision based on treating others in the same way you would like to be treated

client person with whom a real estate agent has a brokerage relationship

closing another term for settlement of a loan or on a property

code of ethics a formalized set of conduct principles for a specific group

cold-calling session members of a real estate office meet to make calls seeking clients to either purchase or sell a home

competitive market analysis (CMA) research of existing market prepared for either seller or buyer to determine appropriate pricing of property

contingency a set period of time in which some specified future event must occur (or not occur) or the contract may be voided

Controlling the Assault of Non-Solicited Pornography and Marketing (CAN-SPAM) federal legislation to limit amount of unwanted emails

counteroffer a response from a seller or buyer that changes the terms of the original offer to purchase

customer person involved in a real estate transaction who is not the client of the agent

designated agent designated by the broker to represent either the buyer or the seller when both the buyer and the seller are clients of the same company

discount broker brokerage firm offering services at a discount

domain name name assigned to internet user

dual agency when both the seller and the purchaser are represented by the same broker

dual agent one agent represents both the seller and the purchaser in the same transaction with equal representation of both clients

due process an established set of procedures to ensure fair and reasonable treatment of all parties involved

ends-based principle making a decision based on doing the greatest good for the most people

English as a second language (ESL) frequent cause of language barrier problems

escalation clause added to contract showing purchaser's willingness to pay more than the offered price when there are competitive contracts presented

ethical dilemma a problem that requires a decision based on what is right or wrong, or in some cases, what is "more" right

ethical paradigm a conflict between two aspects of an ethical decision where there is "right" on both sides

ethics a discipline dealing with what is fair and right

expulsion most severe sanction for violating the Code of Ethics; expels REALTOR® from membership in NAR

Fair and Accurate Credit Transaction Act (FACTA) requires companies dealing with personal information to destroy such information before disposing of it

Fair Housing Act the 1968 legislation protecting the public from discrimination in areas of race, color, religion, and national origin; sex added as a category in 1974; mental and/or physical handicap and familial status added in 1988

familial status a protected class under Fair Housing Act to avoid discrimination against families with children

fee-for-service real estate business model where client picks specific services to be provided for a set fee

fiduciary responsibility responsibility of an agent to provide care, obedience, accounting, and loyalty to the client; replaced in many states today with statutory duties

for sale by owner (FSBO) term used in real estate for properties sold by the owner with no agent

Golden Rule "do unto others as you would have them do unto you"; stated in the New Testament as the standard for treatment of others

good-faith estimate (GFE) form required by RESPA to be given within three business days by the lender to borrowers that enumerates all costs involved in purchasing a home

grievance committee acts similarly to a grand jury; determines whether, if the facts as presented are true, there might be a violation of the Code of Ethics

home inspection an inspection of all major components of a house to identify any potential problems; usually required and paid for by the prospective purchaser

HUD-1 Settlement Sheet required by HUD for all settlements

Internet link way to connect from one website to another on the internet

kickback refers to monies paid for referral without provision of any service

Kidder's paradigms Rushworth Kidder writes about four paradigms where there is "right" on both sides of the problem: Truth Versus Loyalty, Individual Versus Community, Short-Term Versus Long-Term, and Justice Versus Mercy

latent defects defects in the property that are not clearly visible

letter of reprimand sanction for violation of the REALTOR® Code of Ethics; placed in member's file

letter of warning mildest sanction for violation of the REALTOR® Code of Ethics; placed in member's file

limited representative type of agency relationship where only certain specific duties apply

listing agent the real estate licensee who has listed a property for sale

living document one that is continually revised and adjusted according to current usage

MAP Rule regulations regarding advertising of mortgage information

mediation an alternative to arbitration where the parties are able to work out their own solution to the problem

Megan's Law refers to legislation passed in 1996 requiring all states to establish a system for notification to the public when a released sex offender has moved into a community

moral mentor a wise and good person whose opinions are admired

morality principles of right and wrong relating to behavior

Mortgage Bankers Association (MBA) professional organization for mortgage bankers

multiple listing service (MLS) an organized system where brokers in a given area make an offer of cooperation to other brokers to sell their listings

National Association of REALTORS® professional organization for real estate licensees

National Do Not Call Registry Federal Trade Commission (FTC) and Federal Communications Commission (FCC) regulation to prohibit soliciting calls made to those listed on the DNC registry

nonmaterial defects defects that do not actually affect the physical condition of the house

one-stop shopping brokerage firm also provides access to other service providers such as mortgage company, title company, home inspection

Pathways to Professionalism guidelines provided by NAR for better business practice

Platinum Rule "do unto others as they would be done unto"

pocket listing broker does not enter listing into MLS

points each point is one percentage point of the mortgage loan amount charged by lenders to increase their yield

potential conflict of interest perception that the decision maker could be influenced by personal gain or loss from the decision

preamble the introduction to the REALTOR® Code of Ethics

predatory lending lending that unnecessarily forces customers into loans with higher interest rates, higher down payments, and shorter terms of loan

probation member may be placed on probation of membership as sanction due to violation of the REALTOR® Code of Ethics

procuring cause the one who initiated a series of events that led to a successful transaction

Professional Standards Committee group of peer REALTORS® selected to process ethics complaints and requests for arbitration

Professional Standards Hearing Panel group of peers convened to hear an alleged violation of the REALTOR® Code of Ethics

public trust concerns misappropriation of client's fund or fraud resulting in economic harm

real estate licensee one who is licensed by the state to practice real estate

Real Estate Settlement Procedures Act (RESPA) legislation requiring that consumer be made aware of all costs involved in obtaining a mortgage loan and closing on property; requires provision of good-faith estimate and use of HUD-1 statement at settlement; prohibits kickbacks

REALTOR® real estate licensee who is a member of the National Association of REALTORS®

REALTOR® Code of Ethics written in 1913 to promote high ethical standards of conduct for Realtors®; required for membership in the association

rule-based principle making a decision based on established rules and regulations

sanction action taken against a REALTOR® for violation of an article of the REALTOR® Code of Ethics

Secure and Fair Enforcement Mortgage Licensing (SAFE Act) sets standards for loan originators

Securities and Exchange Commission (SEC) registers all real property securities except those limited to within a state or a private offering

selling agent the real estate licensee representing the purchaser

settlement the final closing of the loan and transfer of title to the property

Sherman Antitrust Act legislation prohibiting price-fixing and defined market share

short sale lender is willing to accept less than the actual amount due on a mortgage loan

situational ethics alteration of ethical position to suit particular circumstances

Standards of Conduct part of state regulatory rules and regulations for real estate licensees' behavior

Standards of Practice (SOP) further interpretations or amplifications of individual articles of the REALTOR® Code of Ethics

statutory duties those duties or responsibilities specified in state agency law

stigmatized property property where an event such as murder or suicide has taken place; also supposed presence of ghosts on the property

subprime lending provides loans with higher rates for those with credit issues that create higher risks for lenders

suspension sanction for violation of the REALTOR® Code of Ethics; members suspended from membership in NAR for a set period of time

undisclosed dual agency when an agent has legal responsibility to one party to the transaction but is, in fact, acting on behalf of the other party without disclosure

virtual office real estate office taking advantage of high technology

website individual's information provided on the internet

Notes